Marketing Avengers

SUPERHEROES OF MARKETING JOIN FORCES TO SHARE THEIR SUPERPOWERS WITH YOU

Richard Seppala with
The Marketing Avengers®

Authority Media Group

NEWARK, DE

Authority Media Group
2035 Sunset Lake Rd, Suite B2
Newark, DE 19702
www.authoritymediagroup.com

Ordering Information:

Quantity sales. Special discounts are available on quantity purchases by corporations, associations, and others. For details, contact the "Special Sales
Department" at the address above.

Marketing Avengers / Richard Seppala. —1st ed.

ISBN   978-0-9909955-4-8 paperback
         978-0-9909955-5-5 ebook
         978-0-9909955-6-2 casebound

Library of Congress Control Number: 2017930317

Contents

Marketing Avengers Assemble!

"With great power comes great responsibility."

MANY OF YOU will recognize that famous line of dialogue from the origin story of one of the world's most popular superheroes, Spider-Man, who discovered that, because he had gained incredible powers, he had a duty to help out those in need.

Well, I intend to flip that Spidey script a little. In this book, our mantra is...

"With great power comes great profits!"

Let me explain. The superheroes represented in the forthcoming pages can't fly, shrink, grow, or burst into flames; nor can they throw enchanted hammers or invincible star-spangled shields. None of them have a Fortress of Solitude or a Batcave to hang out in, and I'm pretty sure there aren't any Norse gods among them either. If they are, they aren't talking.

No, all these superheroes are very different from the kinds you see in the cinema – because they're all people who have transformed themselves from mere ordinary mortals into incredibly awesome and extraordinary marketers. And the advice they're about to deliver in the chapters to come is guaranteed to up your ROI (Return on Investment).

How did I gather together all these awesome marketing champions in one amazing book?

Well, you see, I'm kind of a superhero myself (and, by the way, my superpower isn't modesty...). For over 15 years in my super-guise as "The ROI Guy," I've helped rescue business owners and professionals from declining profits, overpowering competitors, and wasteful and expensive marketing that doesn't work, by using cutting-edge technology and automated systems that capture and track leads, instantly calculate the ROI of advertising campaigns, streamline online sales funnels and much, much, more.

While carrying out my ROI Guy duties, I've run across many others who have impressed me mightily with their marketing "super feats." Which got me to thinking – if we can contribute so much individually to people's bottom lines, imagine how much marketing magic we could accomplish if we banded together – and gave everyone all our hard-won secrets in one fell swoop!

Thus was born the idea to create a team of "Marketing Avengers" – a super-group that offered the best and brightest marketing ideas in use today!

Gives you chills, doesn't it?

But all kidding aside, the folks in this book are the real deal. From Facebook campaigns to selling on Amazon, from supersizing online video success to crafting a successful crowdfunding campaign, our Marketing Avengers offer you a wide array of super-strong secret tricks, tips and techniques that will allow you to both power up your profits and lower your marketing costs. Along the way, you'll also get motivational advice from a Navy Seal, mind-altering info from a master hypnotist and new and exciting ways to use such evergreen marketing tactics as direct mail and referrals.

And, like the infomercials like to say, that's still not all!

However, it is enough for this introduction. If you really want to experience the full depth and breadth of all that the Marketing Avengers have to offer, then I invite you to read on – because they're going to share much of their extremely-confidential expertise here for the first time.

You'll find this is an all-star line-up that's definitely unbeatable – especially when it comes to maximizing sales of your products and services in the marketplace!

Richard Seppala
Orlando, Florida

Meet the Sensational Siphon!

By Richard Seppala

I'm proud to say there's a lot of amazing people in this book all talking about amazing marketing techniques. But, at the same time, I don't want to feel left out – I mean, c'mon, I'm the guy who put this whole book together!

So I decided that it's my turn to swoop into action - with what I think is the most super-amazing-astonishing marketing weapon to come along in a long time. And just like only Batman has a Bat-mobile and only Green Lantern has a Power Ring, this baby belongs exclusively to me.

What is it? I am about to tell you all about it – and once we do, we think you're going to be very interested in leveraging this mighty marketing power tool to your profitable advantage. So get ready to meet...Siphon!

WE WOULD VENTURE to say that 99.9999999% of all of you out there reading this chapter have one thing in common: If you have a business, you primarily sell through the internet. These days, on average, 60% of a marketers' time is devoted to digital marketing activities, according to the Smart Insights and Ecommerce Expo. And that's truly mind-blowing, considering it's been less than twenty years since online advertising was even a viable concept.

Now, we don't have to sell you on all the positives of online marketing, but we're going to list a few of them here anyway. It's crazy cheap if you do it right. You have access to massive amounts of leads on a daily basis. It's incredibly easy to update your campaigns and adjust based on what's working and what's not.

But, of course, there are two sides to every story and there are some negatives to internet marketing. And one of the chief downsides of it is the fact that most of the time...you have no idea who the leads are that you're selling to.

And that makes your targeting more than a little difficult.

Now, if you had a primarily brick-and-mortar business, that problem wouldn't be quite as severe. If, for instance, you owned a car dealership, and somebody came in to look over your latest line of vehicles, you have a few ways to size up the potential buyer. How they're dressed. How they speak. How they present themselves.

But if you're, say, a dentist, and somebody visits your website, emails you or responds to a special offer on your Facebook page, you have almost nothing to go on. Can this person only afford a cleaning? Or do they have the bankroll to get a whole smile makeover? How much effort should you put into this anonymous e-lead? And the problem becomes, if you spend too much to market to them, you're throwing money away. If you spend too little...well, it could be you just let a very big fish off the hook.

That's why Richard (aka "The ROI Guy") worked long and hard to pioneer the art of selling to and collecting data on anyone who calls in to your business. But, lately, he's been increasingly frustrated that many of the same techniques he's been able to use with phone numbers haven't been possible in the online marketing arena.

Well, his frustration is over – because we've put together an amazing new system that any business can use to its huge benefit. It's a system that takes all the guesswork out of your internet marketing efforts – and allows you to continually update, refine and maximize your lead targeting and retargeting capabilities until...well, the sky's the limit.

That new system is called Siphon.

The Siphon

At its core, Siphon is a proprietary traffic filtering system. Now, before you reply, "So what?", let us assure you – this system solves so many of your online marketing dilemmas, it's crazy.

Except it's not.

Siphon actually brings sanity to your online marketing efforts – by allowing you to know exactly who's interacting with your various online entry points (website, social media, apps, etc.), identify how potentially profitable those leads might be, and empowering you to market the most effectively to them.

So how does it deliver all that? Well, we're going to go ahead and spell out in this chapter what exactly Siphon can do for you.

Literally.

"S" is for "Smart"

Siphon isn't just a piece of static technology that just delivers the same results, day after day.

No, Siphon is a self-learning system that continually uncovers more information about the traffic coming your way on a daily basis.

For example, if you install it on your website, any visitor to your website must pass through Siphon first – before your homepage even loads. That right there is a big difference between Siphon and other lead-tracking systems. Those other guys usually require the web page to load first and then they use a JavaScript program or something similar to identify a lead. Which means the visitor might get frustrated and leave the site before it does load. Worse yet, their browser might not have the Java plug-in, which means that system doesn't work at all. In Siphon's case, because the visitor hits our system before they even get to your website, load time is not affected.

And it doesn't matter what browser the visitor is using as Siphon's technology is self-contained.

When Siphon goes to work, the first thing it does is try to identify if the website visitor is a real live human like you or me – or a "bot" (which, if you don't know, is short for "web robot," a software application that's sent out to check out various websites for various reasons).

If it is a bot, Siphon will next determine if it's a good bot or a bad bot. If it's bad, it can block it from ever getting near your site again. Maintaining your website and business is demanding enough without having to worry about the increasing amount of threats that exist online today. Siphon will help to prevent these threats from ever reaching your site, letting you have peace of mind knowing your site is protected against the most common attack techniques.

Not only that, but bots and other malicious visitors are the leading causes of fraudulent clicks and impression padding, which can lead to lower returns on advertising campaigns. Siphon is able to identify and ensure real human beings are being shown your content and advertisements. After all, bots aren't going to buy from you – turns out they rarely have credit cards on them! And if it turns out the visitor is a real human being, Siphon then takes steps to figure out if it's a human that might buy from you (How? Hold on - we'll talk about that process in more detail shortly).

The best part? Each time Siphon encounters and identifies an online visitor, it gets smarter. It "learns" through a powerful algorithm which we call the "RiskDecision Algorithm," which constantly adapts and updates itself to ensure that it makes the smartest possible decision in terms of directing incoming traffic. And don't sweat it getting out of control, you're always in charge of what Siphon does with a simple control panel and an easy-to-learn 4-step process.

In other words, no matter how brilliant Siphon becomes, you still get to be the boss.

"I" Is for "Ideal Customer"

We're assuming you've heard of the "80/20" rule. It's also known as "Pareto's Law," after Italian economist Vilfredo Pareto, who did some number-crunching back in the day and discovered that 80% of income in Italy was generated by 20% of the Italian population. Let's hope they spread the pasta around a little more democratically.

Pareto uncovered what seems to be a universal truth that also applies to your marketing efforts: Most of your sales come from a small percentage of consumers out there. So, instead of wasting 80% of your marketing budget on people who won't buy, it's much smarter and profitable to focus most of it on those who will.

The problem: How exactly do you know who those people are?

Siphon is a tool that can help you identify the demographics of those who will spend the most with you – so you can focus on (a) selling more to those specific demographics and (b) double (or maybe even triple) that 20% of your customer base that spends the most on your products and/or services.

In other words, when you find more of the kinds of customers who make you the most money...they help you make even more money.

We call this type of premium lead profile your "Ideal Customer." And when you can identify and market to these Ideal Customers, you'll experience unheard-of response rates – because you're reaching out to leads who are both predisposed to buy from your kind of business, as well as leads who can afford to buy from your business.

Siphon helps you do all that and more. And that brings us to our next letter of the alphabet...

P is for "Psychographics"

We threw around the word "demographics" a lot in the last section. But that term is actually a little misleading – and limiting. The word that really fits is "psychographics."

What's the difference?

Demographic information provides basic facts about consumers; their gender, age, income, marital status and so forth. Psychographics takes this kind of data analysis more than a few steps further – because it also reveals a consumer's hobbies, values, spending habits, etc. This kind of "big data" digs deep to discover how likely a lead is to buy something that your business provides.

You can only effectively reach your target audience when you understand both their demographics and psychographics. The combination of both sets of data helps you zero in on the "Ideal Customer" profile we just discussed – and gives you a detailed snapshot of the leads you should be marketing to most frequently.

This is exactly the kind of information Siphon delivers with each lead – and it's far, far more than Google Analytics or most other systems are capable of. Siphon analyzes 50+ data points of each visitor and then compiles data on which type of consumer would be most receptive to what type of marketing from you. And, as we noted, because Siphon keeps "learning" about each lead and its activity, it can alert you when a lead that fits your Ideal Customer profile shows up – and then deliver contact data on that person so you can continue to market to that person.

Best of all, Siphon delivers psychographic analysis on each lead on a real-time basis, by tracking the IP address of the computer being used by the lead. That means, incredibly enough, it can tell you instantly when a visitor shows up if they are a viable lead!

And that takes us to our next letter of the alphabet...

H is for "Higher ROI and Higher Conversion Rates"

This is where Siphon can really do you a solid.

When it can identify the psychographics of a lead instantly, when it can tell what product or service of yours the lead might be interested in and how likely it is that the lead will buy from you...

...then Siphon can take them to the marketing offer they're most likely to snap up.

In other words, you don't have to send every visitor to your website to the same one-size-fits-all generic home page as everybody else. No, when you can tell in advance what the person might be interested in and what they can afford...well, you can send them to the landing page of your choosing.

Here's a simple example. Let's say you have an online pet supplies site. If Siphon identifies a visitor as a regular buyer of dog food, then it can immediately direct them to a landing page that sells dog products, instead of cat products or a variety of different pet products.

This kind of personalized marketing is what businesses should be doing and, for the most part, aren't – and that's why, according to most statistics, half of marketing budgets are being wasted. They're still trying to do old school marketing – like those advertisers who buy time on television networks and broadcast commercials that act as a shotgun blast at all the different people who happen to be watching that particular program. Those advertisers are paying, in some cases, for millions of eyeballs that have absolutely no interest in what they're saying.

Now – imagine if the technology existed to show a different commercial in every household's televisions, based on psychographic information about those specific residents. That's exactly what Siphon can do with your online traffic!

As we've said, Siphon is able to provide our clients with insight into their visitors before a page is even finished loading. With these advanced metrics, website owners can make business decisions to capitalize on their traffic before their servers are touched. A dental office, for example, can send an older consumer to an implant ad, a younger woman to a cosmetic dentistry landing page and a teenager to a video promoting Invisalign. A business can also direct premium leads to a limited-time, exclusive and compelling offer that would actually disappear forever if they fail to click on the right link in time – creating a must-act-now deal that a lot of leads will be anxious to take advantage of.

And there are other cool ways you can configure Siphon. Let's say you're a law practice in Indiana – and Siphon identifies a visitor to your website as being from Florida. Well, maybe you've set up a referral arrangement with a legal colleague in Tampa. If that's the case, Siphon can send Florida traffic to their website instead of yours – and perhaps that Tampa firm will send Indiana leads to your website in exchange.

Maybe you want to send people clicking to your site from various social media platforms to their own distinct destinations. For instance, someone coming from one of your Facebook offers would be directed by Siphon to a special Facebook-oriented page. Instagram, Twitter...whatever. You can control where each lead goes depending on where they're coming from.

It's all possible because Siphon uses proactive analysis. Other web traffic tracking systems give you visitor information after those visitors have already left the site. By that time, you've lost the chance to maximize the results of their visit; looking at their activity two hours after the fact is closing the barn door after the horse is gone. With Siphon, you can make and program critical marketing decisions in advance and then follow up on the leads' behavior – allowing you to, once again, instantly change or reconfigure how Siphon reacts to those leads the next time around.

Ultimately, all of this refining and experimenting ends up creating a bulletproof online marketing dynamo, one that will consistently continue to elevate your conversion rates and your ROI. The more it learns about each kind of lead and their behavior, the more it will take them to the landing pages and offers that will earn you the most revenue – which will send your ROI soaring.

And not just with your online marketing...

"O" is for "Offline Success"

Here's an important thing to note: Siphon's process of collecting data on leads isn't limited to your website visitors. People emailing you, contacting you through social media, using your app if you have one, even calling you on this ancient device we call "the phone" ...all of these "points of entry" can be used to further discover more Ideal Customers and their contact information. That's because we also have the ability to do what we call "backend analysis" of a customer's database. We can gain data from their email database, their smartphone log database and so forth.

This helps you identify more leads that you can market to not only online, but offline as well. Again, once you understand who your Ideal Customer is, you can use a specific offline marketing technique such as direct mail (which can be still incredibly effective) to great advantage. That's because you no longer have to blow your budget by sending that direct mail piece to an entire zip code or an expensive mailing list you purchase that might not even work for your business. Now, you can create your own mailing list, tailored to your Ideal Customers, which will maximize your ROI, increase your response rate and minimize your campaign cost.

In addition, you can tailor your actual business operation more to your Ideal Customer's liking, once Siphon has helped you identify what that profile wants. You can offer more of what they will buy – and eliminate other products and services that are either profit-neutral or possibly even profit-negative (in other words, what Donald Trump might call a "loser").

The point is, Siphon delivers unassailable marketing information that cuts across all marketing channels and business operations. You will finally have the exact data you need to build the kind of money-making operation you're after. It doesn't matter how successful you've been to this point; the Siphon can make you even more successful, more profitable and more responsive to the kind of customers you want to attract over your company's lifetime. And it can do all that because...

"N" is for "Nothing Better"

You've probably heard from a lot of salespeople selling marketing systems that their technology is "proprietary" – and claim that theirs is the only system in the world that can accomplish certain tasks. We know from experience – and you probably do too – that, many times, all that is just sales hype.

Well, our technology is proprietary – and it is the only system that can do the things we're talking about in this chapter. We know this because we personally developed this technology ourselves with our talented programmer, Shawn Bayer. The code was written and developed in house and we already have a patent in process right now, because we believe we've come up with something truly revolutionary. To our knowledge, no one else has put all the pieces of the puzzle together as we have with Siphon. You might be able to get an element here or an element there with some other program...but this kind of all-powerful all-in-one package? No. Way.

Siphon is one-of-a-kind – and it's ready to go to work for you. Now that you've heard about its amazing super powers, isn't it time to think about putting it into action for your business? If you want to find out more specifics, we invite you to check out the Siphon website at siphoncloud.com to find out more about this powerful new Marketing Avenger – and to contact us for a free consultation.

You'll soon find out, if you haven't guessed already, that Siphon really spells trouble for your competition.

Claiming Your Authority Position

How to Leverage Your Expertise and Power Up Your Profile

By Chuck Boyce

Full Disclosure—I've worked with Chuck Boyce for a number of years. As a matter of fact, he worked with me to put this book together. So, you might say he's partly responsible for assembling all these amazing Marketing Avengers.

Chuck has his own special super power, and that's raising your professional reputation to new heights. His Authority Media Group helps all kinds of entrepreneurs, professionals and coaches become known as THE experts in their fields, giving them the ability to magnetically attract new clients and upsize their money-making potential. And he does that magnificently, because he's THE expert in his field!

So, read on, and you'll discover the secrets of how to power up your profile—just by claiming what Chuck calls "the Authority Position."

- Richard Seppala

BEING AN AUTHORITY IS A YEARLONG BUSINESS.

For example, just before April 15th, you'll see a whole host of tax specialists being interviewed on TV and in newspapers. When summer comes rolling around, you'll find veterans of the travel industry sharing their thoughts on great vacation destinations with the media. Around the holidays, you'll see people skilled in gift-giving start appearing on shows like *Good Morning, America* with suggestions on what to give loved ones for Christmas.

Now, all those experts—and plenty of others in completely different fields—don't have to pay for the incredibly valuable media exposure these appearances give them. Once they're established, they don't even have to put their hand up to be asked to be on national television. No, they are pursued by media producers, news websites and print editors because (a) they have valuable content to share with viewers, listeners and readers and (b) they are *known* and *trusted* figures who have taken what I term as an "Authority Position."

The Authority Position makes them superheroes not only in the media universe, but also, and more importantly for them, to the millions of people who see them being presented as top experts and assume they must be among the best at their business. These experts are perceived as elite and they are treated as elite by their clients, allowing them to command premium prices for their services.

Not only that, but whatever content they generate is highly sought-after. Their books are best-sellers, their websites get millions of hits, their speaking engagements sell out, their ancillary products sell out and they often get shows of their own which can run for years. Think of the billion-dollar business empires that perceived authorities such as Dr. Phil, Dr. Oz and Judge Judy have built up, simply for being known for what they do.

Of course, the three names I just mentioned are at the very top of the heap when it comes to claiming Authority Positions and experiencing massive success as a result. But just imagine enjoying just a *piece* of that massive success by claiming the Authority Position for what you do—and receiving not only all those extra profits, but your own special "celebrity perks" as a result.

Well, you don't have to imagine it, because you can make it happen for you. Whether you're a coach, an entrepreneur, a doctor, a lawyer, or almost any other occupation, you can claim the Authority Position and make it work to your advantage too. And in this chapter, I'm going to explain how you can do just that.

My Path to the Authority Position

In my early years as a business owner, I tried numerous techniques, campaigns, and media in an effort to persuade potential customers to buy my products and services. I spent countless hours and a lot of money attending workshops, conferences and webinars featuring the latest, greatest marketing "secret." In the end, it seemed like that secret always boiled down to this: *prospects buy from people they know, like and trust.*

How could I make that happen? Well, I did the same as most marketers did. I bought ads, both online and offline, which touted how great my company was and featured pretty pictures of our building. Those ads lacked personality, however, and gave no compelling reason for prospects to engage with us. We were just another faceless business, trying to look bigger than we were and we got lost as so many others do in the overwhelming deluge of today's marketing messaging.

Then, around five years ago, I came across a marketing program that had as its mandate to make its clients into "celebrities." This seemed a little crazy—I wasn't Brad Pitt or Tom Cruise—and I felt more than a little uncomfortable becoming the spokesperson and "face" of my business. However, I made the investment and worked through the program. The results included a bestselling book, impressive print media mentions, and appearances on network TV. All of this stuff looked cool on my office walls, but, I had to wonder, was it really going to help?

The short answer is, it did.

Because this program enabled me to create an online profile that trumpeted me as an expert, it completely transformed people's perceptions of me when they Googled my name. Instead of just my website and LinkedIn profile coming up, the public instead saw a carefully curated series of links featuring videos, articles, and media mentions, all featuring me and all granting me the Authority Position. And the sum total of those impressive links instantly made me seem more trustworthy and valuable to the prospects who saw them.

The more I saw the amazing results of this program, the more I thought about offering this service on my own. I could finetune the problems I saw with the program I went through and offer my own improved version to other professionals and entrepreneurs.

That's how my Authority Media Group came to be.

One of my first clients was IRS Tax Attorney Darrin T. Mish, Esq. (GetIRSHelp.com), who runs a small, profitable tax law practice in Tampa, Florida. His market is very competitive—he's up against huge firms that spend tons of cash on national TV, radio, print and online advertising. But Darrin, with my help, went ahead and claimed his position of authority—and wrote several books about dealing with tax issues, several of which have been Amazon Best Sellers.

His results were just as positive as mine. He regularly gets calls from prospects who read one of his books they discovered on Amazon books and decided he was the guy they wanted to help them solve their tax problems. Darrin told me that it's very common for these kinds of prospects to practically plead with him to take on their case, because the book showcased his experience and expertise in dealing with the IRS.

Why? Because, by occupying an Authority Position, he completely changed the dynamic of his new client interactions. Instead of him having to persuade prospects that he was the right lawyer for their tax problem, he now had prospects trying to convince *him* to take them on as clients. He's no longer chasing new business—it's chasing him!

Positioning Yourself for Prominence

Think you're not worthy of taking the Authority Position?

Well, you're not alone. The biggest hurdle for many thinking about taking this big step is that they suffer from what's called "imposter syndrome." They feel they're not smart enough for this process and that nobody would want to listen to them anyway.

Everyone, however, with some expertise knows a lot more about their field than someone who's not in that line of work. And they have a lot to offer in the form of helpful advice and information that applies to their lives. You can be a plumber or construction worker and still be able to assume an Authority Position, just by talking knowledgably about all the stuff you understand and take for granted, just because it's a part of your everyday work.

If you think you have imposter syndrome, here's a good way to get over it. Find a notable expert in your industry, ideally one that appears regularly on mass media like broadcast television. Watch as they dispense their advice to the callers and audience participants. Then, ask yourself:

- Was this person smarter than you? (Probably not)
- Would you give the same or better advice? (Probably so)

Here's what it comes down to: An industry expert has to "water down" the information they give to audiences and keep things simple. If they get too inside about their expertise, people won't know what the heck they're talking about. So, even if you haven't mastered highly complex aspects of your business, it doesn't matter as long as you fully understand the basics the public wants to know about.

What *does* matter is if you have the desire to use your knowledge and expertise to help your prospective and existing clients. I'm going to assume you *do* have that desire, otherwise you wouldn't be good at what you do. That desire is all you need in order to claim your Authority Position.

Preparing for Authority Positioning

There are a few steps you need to take in order to get ready to create the perception of being an expert. Let's go through a few of them in this section.

Maintain a strong brand across all social media outlets

Anyone who claims an Authority Position needs to ensure their online identity consists of branding that is (a) **consistent** and (b) **professional**. If you don't look like a polished expert, people are not going to accept you in the role. So, if you're on Facebook, Twitter, etc. (and you should be, if you're going to follow through with this), you want to make sure all your social profiles all reflect your Authority Position in a manner that's not amateurish.

That process begins with using a professionally-done profile photo of yourself. A company mug shot, an overly-cropped vacation photo, a webcam selfie or (the worse sin of all) no photo at all won't do, nor will a picture of your dog or cat. For maximum impact, consider having a series of dynamic profile photos that you rotate on a regular basis. Periodically changing your headshot will cause you to show up in the social media feeds of your connections in a non-obtrusive way.

Another great way to polish your social media presence is to model it after some other expert who stands out to you and/or has a huge following. This person doesn't have to be an expert in the same industry as you, but their branding should be similar enough so that it will resonate with your specific niche. Also, pay close enough attention to the *type* of content they create, the frequency with which they post it and the tone they use. Odds are, if their social media strategy is paying big rewards for them, it will do the same for you.

Put yourself in the media mix

The truth is, anyone can *say* they're an authority. But what really cements your expert status is having other people vouch for you.

After all, both Dr. Oz and Dr. Phil, who I mentioned earlier, owe their careers to Oprah Winfrey granting them an Authority Position.

Third-party verification is crucial to your Authority Position, and the best way to get that ball rolling is to get yourself featured on other media platforms, including websites and publications that are specific to your industry. When you're quoted in someone else's article on an established media platform, you're instantly seen as a recognized expert who wants to share helpful information that everyone can use. Even if you're just featured on someone else's blog, it's something you can promote and point to as evidence of your Authority Position.

Of course, the bigger the medium, the better—because appearing on, say, local affiliates of ABC, NBC, CBS and FOX will add immensely to this "halo effect." When potential clients check out your website and see those powerful media logos, it will rocket your star power in their eyes—because if these big-time outlets trust your Authority Position that much, then you must be important.

Never underestimate the power of *"As Seen On..."* or *"As Featured In..."* to push buyers off of the fence!

Publish and distribute original content

Your content needs to reflect your Authority Position, so it should always aim to *educate and advocate* for your prospects. And remember, there are many forms you can use to present that content. Blogs, videos, podcasts, short (but informative) tweets, visual memes, all of them can serve a specific purpose in presenting your expertise. Use whatever forms are most comfortable for you as well as most attractive to your prospects.

Ideally, the content you share should contain ideas that you are passionate about in a format that allows you to create it quickly, consistently and with a high degree of quality. Don't worry about achieving perfection with your content—you want to bond on a human level with your audience, and that means if you cough in the middle of a video or spell something wrong on a blog, it's not such a big deal. What *is* a big deal is making sure your content is accurate, fresh and interesting to the people you want to reach.

One more note: Avoid constant self-promotion and learn the art of the "humble brag." Prospects want you to deliver value to them, not to yourself. Of course, you'll want to make some offers along the way, just don't make it a huge part of your messaging or you'll lose people. As you develop your social media voice, you'll figure out the right balance.

Publish or perish

Authority begins with the word "author." So, if you're really serious about claiming your Authority Position...think about writing your own book.

BusinessWeek surveyed a group of entrepreneurs and business owners who had written books and found that 96% of them indicated that they realized a significant positive impact on their business by writing a book and would recommend the practice to others.

A book does so much for an author that it's been called "the best business card in the world." That's because having a book instantly makes your prospects think you're a top-tier expert who's extremely credible. And having a *best-selling* book makes you nearly untouchable (by the way, it's not as hard to achieve this status as you might think). This perception automatically rubs off on your business and opens up a ton of opportunities that you might never have realized otherwise. Doors that seemed welded shut will now be opened by others on your behalf.

And the thing is, it's not that hard to create a book. Especially these days.

You might be intimidated just by having to come up with all that content. But, odds are, you've already created a lot of it in other forms. Have you ever given a speech? Presented at a networking event? Have you generated a white paper? Written a series of blogs or articles? Done a series of YouTube videos containing your expertise? All of these types of content (and others as well) contain at least the beginnings of your book content and can certainly get you started in the right direction.

By the way, don't think about writing a book as a money-making venture, except from the standpoint of how it will expand your existing business. You're not going to make a million from sales. You may not even make thousands. But you WILL boost your Authority Position.

The Big Reveal

Finally, I want to share a big secret with you. It involves what I was just talking about, publishing your own book. And it involves putting together that book in such a way that *you only have to write one chapter*. Not only that, but it delivers the amazing benefit of positioning yourself as the *leader* of a group of authorities in your field of expertise.

What kind of book could do all that? The same kind of book you're reading this chapter in!

Marketing Avengers was my friend Richard Seppala's idea. Richard has been a master marketer for over two decades, so he doesn't need to position himself as an authority, he already is one. But he wants to keep that position strong and healthy, so he likes to put out a book with his name on it on a regular basis. The problem is, because he's already written a few best-sellers, he's used up a lot of his content and was worried that he didn't have enough left to say to fill up another book.

His solution?

Gather together *other* marketing experts to contribute chapters of their own to really give the reader a ton of bang for their buck.

Now, this accomplishes two big goals for Richard (besides providing all that extra value). One, he doesn't have to write the entire book himself and two, he doubles down on his Authority Position by gathering a whole bunch of other experts under his umbrella.

You can easily do the same. Let's say you're a business coach who wants to do a similar kind of book. Well, you can gather respected experts on various subjects that are an integral part of your coaching process with clients and have them each do a chapter on their specialty. You provide an introduction, maybe an afterword, and then a chapter or two of your own advice for entrepreneurs.

Result? Instant credibility and the perception that you network with (and have the benefit of the counsel of) the leading business experts in the country. It's a win-win for everybody involved, but no one gets more out of it than you. Credibility is critical to any successful coach and you've just earned it in spades.

Battling Your Inner "Marketing Monster"

With Sean Stephenson

Internationally-famous speaker. Therapist. Best-selling author. Friend of Presidents. TV star. Viral video sensation. Yes, Sean Stephenson is an amazing phenomenon who's not only experienced massive success in virtually every endeavor he's attempted, but has also brought an incredible amount of hope and inspiration to millions across America.

But what makes him even more amazing is the fact that Sean almost didn't survive his own birth.

For those of you who don't know Sean's story, he was born with a rare genetic disorder called osteogenesis imperfecta, or "brittle bone" disease. Almost all of his bones were broken during delivery and pain was a constant companion during his childhood. Today, Sean is confined to a wheelchair – but his intelligence and his spirit remain boundless, as do his marketing skills.

I'm very proud he chose to participate in our Marketing Avengers book – because this guy is one very real superhero we all can learn from. Here's our conversation.

- Richard Seppala

You began to market yourself when you were still in your teens. Was it hard for you to get out there originally, considering your disability?

My experience with marketing took place at a young age because I realized that marketing is whatever efforts you take to grab somebody's attention. And I was *born* with that. I began thinking, "Wait a minute. Everybody's staring at me and I'm not having to do anything to get this attention. *What can I do with this attention?*"

Honestly, it was probably the capitalist in me that keyed in on this at first, and I started thinking about it as far back as grade school and junior high. It wasn't until high school that I started taking action to capitalize on it. I looked around and saw that everyone in my school was doing something to stand out. Whether they're spiking their hair and getting piercings, trying to win basketball games or math competitions, or just getting in trouble and get kicked out of class, everybody's doing something different to get attention. But I don't have to - everybody *already* knows who I am. I can skip that step in this lifetime.

That freed me up to go to the next level in marketing – what was I going to do with that attention? If somebody put a megaphone in your hand and everywhere you went, your voice carried over everybody else's, at some point you would start to ask the question, "What should I be saying with this megaphone?" Because attention by itself is pretty boring, it's trivial. So, at some point, you have to say, "I need something from this."

I saw there were two ways to utilize the attention I was getting. One was for selfish purposes – and I actually think that's fine, when it's kept in good balance with the second way, which is supporting others. In high school, I put those two together when I was asked to speak at another high school about what it's like to have a disability, what it's like being born as an attention-getter. And I had so much fun with that audience, which was made up of all kids my age. They paid me 75 dollars for one hour of my time and in the early 90's, that much money made you feel like the richest man in Babylon. You could buy video games, a lot of candy, a nice jacket, whatever.

But that was just a start. I didn't fully understand marketing until I got to college. That's where I started to realize, "Wow! I know that when people are staring at me, if I put a message to it, I can get paid seventy-five dollars an hour. What if I do *more* things to get more attention? What if I actually go above and beyond my speeches? What if I start doing things to get attention in places where I'm not even located? Like sending out flier, postcards, and emails?" Later, of course, that list would grow to include Google video, YouTube videos, Facebook, Twitter, Snapchat...it turned into a progression. It was me figuring out, 'Wow, there is this thing called marketing where I can clone myself to get people's attention even when I'm not physically there."

What did you study in college?

Political science. During my time in college, I worked for a US Congressman in Capitol Hill, and I worked for a US president in the White House, and fell in love with the experience of human relationships. The top political people on the planet are the ones who understand that everything you ever wanted comes through a relationship. And that applies to marketers too. You should have a relationship with a customer through your messaging. That was an important lesson to learn.

When I got out of college, I still had a thirst to understand more about marketing, so I began seeking out marketing mentors, because they were the best of the best in understanding how to build those kinds of relationships with customers. I'm talking about people like Joe Polish, Richard Branson, Jay Abraham, all these different individuals who understood the importance of creating those relationships through storytelling. Really good marketers are storytellers.

You can even relate marketing to dating, which is what I did in my mid-to-late twenties. It's no different in a way, because when you want to get into a relationship, whether it's for a lifetime or just one night, you have to first *get the attention of that person*. It's all about attracting people, whether it's a customer or a potential romantic interest. It's about bringing somebody in to see the best sides of you.

I mean, the greatest marketing takes something that is usually ordinary and makes it sound extraordinary.

And people respond to that kind of messaging, they actually crave it. Science has proven through brain scans that the "pleasure center" of the mind lights up more when someone opens the tin foil on the top of the yogurt container than when they actually eat it. Jerry Seinfeld actually has a routine about it. He says something like, "Let's be honest. We love buying stuff. It's the stuff that's already here that we get pretty disappointed with."

It's more about the message then the actual product.

Yes, it's the dopamine rush we get from novelty, something new.

A lot of what you talk about concerns how to overcome insecurities. How does that play out with marketing?

For me, I'm always looking now to slay my inner marketing monster, which comes full circle to insecurity. Most people have a monster that lives inside of them, that tells them, no one wants your book, no one wants your speech, no one wants your hair salon, no one wants your stupid idea, whatever it may be. That's your inner marketing monster talking. It gets you to think, "Well, if I don't tell anyone about this and it doesn't sell, then I'm not going to have to feel like a loser - because I never did anything about it in the first place."

If you don't try, you don't fail.

Yes, take it back to dating - if I don't go and talk to that girl, then she can't reject me. And that means I never got rejected. Same principle. So I'm inspired to help people slay their own marketing monsters, so they can realize that, in business, those that make it are usually not the most talented, they're the most *persistent*. In a world where there are a lot of choices, we pay attention to the ones that are constantly coming at us.

The commercial you hear a million times a day is the one you remember.

Exactly. Now, as I get older, I'm realizing the importance of closing the deal. If I tell you about a program ten times, but I never tell you how much it is and never ask you to buy it, then why did I just do all that marketing? Yes, I understand a lot about marketing, we have over twenty-two different things that we do to market our products and services. But, it's important to remember at the end of the day, you've got to ask for the sale.

What do you think works, in terms of making that sale?

This is what I've learned from studying the Greats, just from reading their work: *What you're delivering has to be so irresistible that people feel like idiots for not buying it.* When you give somebody ten times the value of what they paid, they never feel like they were cheated. So I want my customers telling me, "Sean, you're undercharging." I want them saying, "Please raise the fee. It's way too valuable for the price." That's when I know I'm doing my job, because I'm getting the people to see so much value, price isn't in the discussion. The sooner I can get someone into that dialogue, the better.

To get to that point, a marketer has to be an optimist. Successful marketers don't believe in failure; they believe in *testing*. A successful marketer doesn't come back and say, "We failed that launch. We only had a five percent conversion." They say, "We had a five percent conversion. How can we get to seven?" That's why I love NLP (Neuro Linguistic Programming), where they like to say, "There is no failure, there's only feedback." Almost every major successful launch that I've heard of, whether it was with a product, a service or entertainment, it didn't come out of the gate intact. It got tweaked. It got changed. It got refined. But you never hear about that.

In today's competitive and cluttered online landscape, what do you do to stand out with your marketing?

Our biggest online marketing appeal is through viral video content. I've studied a lot about video and looked at what are the key core elements to videos that go viral, which, to me, is a video that gets anything over a million views within a certain time period. I've had videos that have over a million views, but it took two years to get to that point – that's not really viral. However, earlier this year, we had a video, "2 Minutes with Sean," that went extremely viral – it was averaging a million views an hour for the first two and a half days it was posted and wound up at around 68 million views when it finally started to taper off.

But that's only part of the story. What was wild was that this one video then got downloaded and re-uploaded, so it was seen over 150 million more times around the world. People were translating it and posting it on their own channels – they were capitalizing on my video because they knew it would get a lot of views and bring them more exposure to their own stuff. And that was fine with me, because it's a win for me too.

How does that kind of exposure help you?

In the business of professional speaking, which is one of the hats I wear, your fee is determined by several factors, one of which is how well-known you are. And if 200 million people know who you are, that makes you worth X number of dollars at a speaking engagement; the potential audience has already heard of you and that makes you what they call a draw, you automatically attract interest. And if you can become a draw, that is a good thing.

I worked and worked for twenty-two years at marketing myself. And I watched how, even within the last year, conferences would never feature my name on their tickets. Now, however, after that video, they're putting me up there with much bigger names, like Tony Robbins, because they know hundreds of millions of people now know who I am and enjoyed what I did in the video.

What other marketing is important to you these days?

I've spent a lot of time in what I call "advocate marketing," where I've gotten access to 22 advocates, people that are very well connected in different industries. They're the kind of people who are so busy, they don't need me, they don't need my attention – but, if I pick up a phone, I have a good enough relationship with them that they will happily take my call. They're what I would call world thought leaders, influencers, heads of industry, people that the general populace wouldn't know of, but might be only one phone call away from anyone from the Dalai Lama to the President of the United States.

It's a powerful network.

Yep. And I paid good money to some people to have them in my network. Others just do it because they followed me for years and love what I do. What I provide to them is value that I trickle on them throughout the years. If somebody is my advocate, my therapy services are on call for them, absolutely free of charge. They can call me at three in the morning and say, their best friend is suicidal. Can I get out of bed and talk to them? And the answer is always yes. Because my advocates are people that, with one opportunity, can put me in the head of a line that would take me decades to reach otherwise. In terms of marketing, instead of the shotgun approach, I'm using more of a sniper rifle. These individuals can get me anywhere, anytime, at any speed. If anything, I need to be prepped and ready for those moments that I get the call from an advocate. I can literally get a call from someone who will say, "Oprah wants you to get on her jet with her and discuss weight loss." And I need to be ready for that.

From my side, advocate marketing can be something as simple as reading a book, highlighting the best parts, and mailing it to an advocate with a note saying, "I know you don't have time to read this whole thing, but check out these twenty top lines, I thought they would be of value to you." It could be something as simple as finding out your advocate's daughter's favorite musician is Justin Bieber and buying her tickets, so her parents can go to a concert with her. It could be finding out the advocate's spouse's favorite wine and going to the vineyard and shipping a case. It's figuring out what signifies value for them, what do they care about, what's their favorite charity. One of my advocates identified somebody they wanted to befriend, and they went out and raised a million dollars for that person's charity. That person, of course, had to then acknowledge them because of that huge sum of money. When you help the people that have what you want get more of it, you naturally get lifted up the ladder with them.

I'm very careful as to who I select to be in my advocate group, because I want to make sure my values are aligned with theirs. When you get connected to somebody that has a different set of values than yours, they start bringing shady opportunities to you and then you find out the hard way you've made a mistake. We live in a visual society where one picture of your genitalia sent to the wrong person can end up burning down a lifetime of hard work. I don't ever like to play moral police, but I know they exist. There will be times where people will be like, "Hey Sean, why don't you go out to a strip club with us? First of all, I'm happily married. Even if my wife and I were cool with that idea, which we're not, we live in a cell phone generation where everybody has a camera, and the next thing you know, somebody takes a picture and it's like "Oh, Sean's not happy with his marriage, that's why he's at a strip club." Nobody wants to hear that maybe I was there because of a bachelor party, they're more interested in the scandal aspect. So why give them that ammunition?

Because of my advocate marketing, I do a lot less mass-marketing nowadays then I did when I was younger, because I'm more clearly targeting who I need. My social media is more of a shotgun approach, because I'll do a video or post, hit "send" and it goes to the approximately 900,000 people following me on Facebook. With all those people, that activity might not mean anything, but it also might lead to a $20,000 speech, or a gig executive-coaching, or somebody buying a copy of my book and loving it so much, they then buy 2000 copies for their company. You don't know where your efforts will take you.

ABM is my motto: Always be Marketing. I always take, at least, on a slow week, five to seven requests for podcasts, or articles, or books like this. Because who knows where my voice and likeness will end up echoing through their channels. If I have time on my calendar, we carve it out because it's another form of marketing.

The idea is to get yourself out there and connect with other people.

Exactly.

Do you have a final message for all of our Marketing Avengers reading this chapter?

I'd like to go back to that inner marketing monster I talked about earlier. The biggest thing that eats every human being alive, if they don't stay ahead of it, is their insecurities, that feeling like you're not enough in some way. When you think you're not calm enough, smart enough, pretty enough, rich enough...whenever you feel like you're at some kind of disadvantage compared to others.

What I teach people is how to create a lifestyle where you no longer feel deficient. The way to do that is through self-care, it's the key to lowering insecurities. Really good self-care builds your happiness and your sanity, and a person who is happy and sane is unstoppable. The problem is the opposite, when you're not happy and not sane, when you feel like you're losing your mind and you feel dark and depressed. That's where the insecurities pull up out of nowhere and pull you in.

I have a simple thing I do that I recommend other marketers do. It's a list that I call your "When Life Works List." And it contains a series of 16 action items that, if I only do four of them a day, you and no army can make me feel insecure. They include things like, hydrate, exercise, meditate, pray, get good sleep, do proper hygiene and grooming, stay organized, eat vegetables, read and review good materials about mind, body and spirit, connect with your advocates, link up and spend time with your significant other, review your goals, plan out your day on paper, spend time learning from young souls like your children or nieces and nephews, and create new content. I especially like that last one, because I believe you feel closest to your Creator when you are creating. I'm constantly thinking about which of these I'm going to do on any given day to nourish my own well-being. Because when I do the self-care action items, my insecurities don't show up and stop me from doing what needs to be done.

Many thanks again to Sean Stephenson for his illuminating marketing (and life) insights. Find out more about Sean and his inspirational message at seanstephenson.com.

.

Becoming a Great Video Marketer

Six Words to Success

By Ian Garlic

Looking for a real Internet marketing hero? Look no further than the incredible, amazing and definitely mighty Ian Garlic, who's been delivering outstanding online results for his clients for almost a decade now, by vanquishing the competition through cutting-edge tactics utilizing SEO, social media and web design.

Oh – and one more thing. Another one of Ian's specialties is video marketing, which is becoming more and more of a game-changing tool in online marketing success. But to really capture that success, you have to do more than talk into a camera about how great you are for a couple of minutes; you have to tell an effective story that will hook viewers instantly. How do you make that happen? Read on and Marketing Avenger Ian will give you the inside scoop!

- Richard Seppala

VIDEO ISN'T JUST AN UP-AND-COMING marketing tool anymore. More and more, it's an established necessity. If you check out any recent statistics on the use of video, you'll quickly discover that it boosts conversion rates through the roof, no matter what industry uses it. It's becoming more and more prevalent in social media platforms such as Facebook, Twitter and Pinterest as well. In 2015, online video account for four times the views as websites and email *combined*.

Not only that, but now, thanks to mobile devices, online video now goes everywhere your customers go. More people are buying on smartphones than desktops or laptops now, and they're no doubt out there Googling the kind of content you can provide in marketing videos. As a matter of fact, YouTube is now the second most-used search engine on the Internet.

As with anything else, however, the more widespread online video becomes, the harder it is for your message to stand out from the crowd. In the past, you could get away with simply shot talking heads addressing the camera with long and rambling speeches about how great your product is. Now is the time to look beyond those kinds of primitive techniques and begin to use proven and effective storytelling techniques to make sure you not only catch people's attention – but you also get them to *respond and buy*.

Situation Marketing

Today, it's easier than ever to quickly create a professional-looking marketing video to market yourself or whatever you're selling. Unfortunately, it's also never been easier to have that video get completely lost in the massive online content churned out daily by consumers and businesses alike. That's why it's increasingly difficult to be a great video marketer in this overcrowded climate. But it still can be done, and, in this chapter, I'm going to show you how.

Let's start with the premise that "Good is the enemy of great" when it comes to online video marketing. A "good" video has trouble making its content stand out. A "good" video, used in every social media platform, broadcasting the exact same message, quickly proves that one size does *not* fit all. A "good" video that tries to appeal to everyone often appeals to no one - because it doesn't seem relevant to his or her personal or professional circumstances.

In contrast, *great marketing videos market to specific situations.* That process begins with the marketer first identifying and then targeting the product or service's "Ideal Client," rather than everyone in the world; an avatar that represents the person most likely to buy their product or service – and then it's up to the marketer to present a situation that their Ideal Client can connect to in a meaningful manner.

Why a situation? Because when it comes to decision-making, it's situations that sway us the most. Who you are as a marketer has only a very slight (.3 maximum) correlation to a client decision; situations dictate our behavior more than anything else. There's tons of scientific proof to back up this statement.

For example, seminary students were once recruited for a study. First they were schooled and quizzed on being a "Good Samaritan," someone who would help a stranger in need in the way the parable in the Bible teaches. Then these students were told to go to another building to continue their education. On the way, a man, planted by the research team, was slumped in an alleyway, moaning and coughing, clearly in need of some care. Overall, however, *only 40%* of the students offered some help to the victim. In low-hurry situations, 63% helped, medium-hurry 45% and high-hurry 10%. In other words, the more intense the situation, the more the students went against their beliefs and ignored the man in need. The situation dictated their behavior.

In another famous study, the Milgram shock tests, college students were asked to administer increasingly painful shocks to subjects. Because they were in a situation where authority figures were telling them what to do, a very high proportion of them were prepared to obey, even if apparently causing serious injury and distress. Again, they predicated their behavior on the situation, not their personal beliefs.

Powerful situations cause us to focus as nothing else can. If you can bring a powerful situation to life, one that relates directly to your Ideal Client and hits them where they live, your marketing video will be *magnetic.*

How do you zero in on the right situation? Let's talk about that next.

The Most Important Story

The most important story you have to tell with your video is your Ideal Client's story. When you can understand the life situation that will work best to sell to them, you're on your way to video marketing success.

The way to reach that understanding? Simple. Write their story. We do that with our clients at authenticWEB by having a Situational Storyboard Marketing Session. We go through and identify their Ideal Client, and then we storyboard that Ideal Client's story (you can see examples of this at:

IanGarlic.com/lessons/storyboard-marketing

We set a timer for 60 minutes and create storyboard panels, each of which represents a scene in the life of the Ideal Client. These sessions are almost always a big game changer for our clients, because they end up forcing themselves to see the world through that Ideal Client's eyes.

And that's the start of a successful marketing effort.

One you've identified the right situation for your marketing purposes, you have two more steps to take:

Step 1: Provide value within the context of that situation. Once you've put yourself in your Ideal Client's shoes, it should be easy to find a way in your video to provide authentic value for them, most likely by solving a problem for them or by offering significant information that will help with the situation.

Step 2: Decide what you want them to do next. This isn't necessarily trying to get them to buy at this point. The true definition of "conversion" is just getting someone to take the next step, whatever you want that next step to be. It could just be getting them to visit your Facebook page, checking out some content on your website or getting their email address added to your list (or some combination of the above). How big a conversion you want to go for is dependent on how strong a relationship you establish, which is what we're going to discuss next.

The Six Most Important Words to Success

When it comes to Situation Marketing, there are six important words to learn and abide by, if you want to have success in video marketing. Those six words come in two sets of three, and here's the first set:

Know, Like, Trust

It's a time-honored axiom that you as a marketer must create a bond with your intended marketing recipient. How strong a bond that ends up being depends on how far up the "Know, Like, Trust" ladder you can take your Ideal Client. Obviously, just knowing who you are as a marketing is the bottom rung, following ascending to (hopefully) liking you and then finally, at the top of this relationship ladder, actually trusting you to deliver on your promises.

The rule of thumb is, the bigger the conversion you are asking for, the closer that potential client must climb to "Like" and "Trust." If, for example, I'm asking you to head over to my Facebook page and check out a short video, you probably have to know me and maybe like me a little – but you certainly don't have to have a lot of trust invested in me at that point. However, if I want to ask you to give me your email address and watch a long half-hour video from me, then I have to build up a whole lot of trust from you first. First of all, I'm asking for a lot of your time, second of all, I'm asking for something private, your email address, that could open you up to a whole lot of spam or random marketing emails you may not want.

Obviously, it's in your best interests to take your leads all the way up this relationship ladder to the "Trust" level. That takes time, however, so don't expect too much too soon or your conversions won't happen.

Wants, Needs and Alibis

As you move up the "Know, Like, Trust" ladder, you're going to want to use videos to create bigger and bigger conversions. In order to do that, you're going to have to create situations that address our next three words, "Wants, Needs and Alibis."

To initially get someone's attention, you're going to first have to address "Wants." Let's say you've built a new kind of food prep software program that helps people eat the healthiest, most nutritious food possible while still taking taste into account. What kinds of "Wants" might that product satisfy? Well, most people *want* to lose weight and stay in shape – and those are two pretty powerful desires to key into.

Your next step is to zero in on situations these kinds of people frequently face. Imagine someone unhappily doing their Monday morning scale reading of their weight after a weekend of pigging out. Or someone planning for a beach vacation, by putting on their bathing suit and viewing the not-so-attractive results in a full-length mirror. These would be easy videos to produce and would be very effective; using these kinds of situational "Wants" is a way to get people to *know* you and begin to take them up the ladder towards "Like" and "Trust."

That takes us to a second stage, where we now address these potential buyers' "Needs." If we've correctly positioned ourselves as an expert in the field we're selling in, we have the credibility to tell people what they *need* to fulfill their "Wants." This only works if people already know us and are starting to like us. Think about it: If you didn't know me and were a little overweight, you wouldn't want me suggesting a food planning app, would you? However, if you now know and like me, we can talk about the importance of meal planning, the easiest way to do it, and allow me to suggest my app. This, in turn, will make them feel like this app is one of their "Needs."

Finally, we have to overcome our potential buyers' "Alibis." In the case of our imaginary food planning app, the potential buyer knows they WANT to look great at the beach, they know they have the NEED to change their lifestyle and eat healthier...but now they may not feel they have the time, willpower or budget to make that happen! These kinds of excuses for not meeting their "Wants" and "Needs" are their "Alibis."

That's why your next video marketing move is to address those Alibis and let your leads know your product is helping them *overcome* them. That builds up trust, because you're showing you understand why they can't lose weight – and that you're able to remove those obstacles with your product.

Wants, Needs, Alibis. Every time you successfully use a situation to video market your product or service, you're also creating opportunities for viewers to "Know, Like, and Trust" you – as well as deal with their "Wants, Needs and Alibis." You just have to decide how much you want to do to develop your relationship with your leads – and what action you want them to take at the end of the video.

Why Video?

Maybe you think I'm so gung-ho on video marketing because people hire me to help them do it. It's true, but the reason I love video so much has nothing to do with money. I've been successful with SEO, websites and social media and know how to be successful without video.

The truth is I really believe video is the best way to market. Video allows you to tell a story visually, just like a great movie – and there's no better way to bring a situation to life. It allows you to show yourself at your best and also to attract the people most likely to buy your message. When we provide value as our authentic selves, through authentic stories, we fulfill our purpose – and video accomplishes all that and more. If I can help one other person fulfill their purpose – and even provide value to one other person, then, in a small way, I have changed two lives.

And what could be better than that?

I'd also like to stress that, while I have learned plenty from making thousands of videos, you don't need a ton of experience (or equipment for that matter) to start providing value through video. In fact, you could download the YouTube app and, within a few minutes, immediately start making your own videos with real value.

Remember also that you have more value than just your product, and you can start providing that value while telling *your* story. Think you don't have one? I promise that you do. I have filmed hundreds of entrepreneurs and have yet to find one without a compelling story. You just have to find a way to relate your story to your Ideal Client.

If you haven't done video before, you're probably a little scared and a little overwhelmed. You don't need to be. Take action by understanding your Ideal Client and uncovering the situations that will provide a winning strategy that will improve with each technological evolution. That way, you'll have no need to worry about the next forthcoming platform, but be excited for it - as it will provide you a new opportunity to connect on a deeper level, provide more value and cut through the noise and the clutter.

Selling On-Camera

The 5 "E's" of Effective Video Communication

By Forbes Riley

Few Marketing Avengers have mastered their super power as expertly as international award-winning TV host, health & fitness expert, and Creator of the SpinGym, Forbes Riley. Forbes is the consummate early-adapter, always having her finger on the pulse of "what's next" and leveraging that in front of global audiences, pioneering multiple platforms in front of a camera. She starred in America's first reality show, "Gotch" for Fox, hosted the first ESPN X-games, launched the first fitness product TV sales platform "Fit-TV" with Body by Jake and has generated more than $2.5 billion in television sales revenue over her career as a powerful presence in the infomercial and home shopping television arenas.

Forbes' career also includes a prolific acting resume through Broadway, film and television. She has appeared on ESPN, TLC, Animal Planet, ABC Family, Hallmark Channel, E! Entertainment

Television, HSN, QVC UK, "Forbes Living" on WE-TV, "The Doc-
tors" on CBS, the hit TV show "24" on Fox and more than 2 dozen
feature films.

Today, Forbes spends her time producing and hosting TV shows,
writing books, running her international fitness empire based
around her best-selling SpinGym system (which has already sold
more than 1.5 million units) and speaking on stages inspiring other
entrepreneurs, and businesses at all levels.

Forbes is also committed to giving back in her career. As such, she
has developed innovative curricula, traveling the United States and
hosting exclusive clinics, mentoring and teaching Masterminds that
involve her branded techniques about the perfect pitch and master-
ing video marketing. Thousands of celebrities, executives, entrepre-
neurs and other influencers, innovators and leaders have benefited
from her knowledge, passion and generosity. Her super power? See-
ing the very best in others and bringing it out in them. Her motto:
Dream It, Believe It, Achieve It.

Clearly Forbes Riley is Marketing Avenger who's flying high and
changing lives... and now, here's Forbes with some high-level video
marketing wisdom.

- Richard Seppala

How important is video in online marketing these days? Here are a
few powerful facts:

- **74% of all internet traffic** in 2017 will be video
- **52%** of marketing professionals worldwide name video as
  the type of content **with the best ROI**
- **65%** of video viewers watch **more than ¾ of a video**
- Video in email can **boost open rates by 20%** and **increase
  click-through rates by two to three times**
- Using the word "video" in email subject lines **boosts open
  rates 19%, click-through rates by 65%** and **reduces unsub-
  scribes by 26%**

Video is clearly becoming the dominant form of marketing media,
and that's why it's critical for any Marketing Avenger to learn how to
script and produce the most compelling video content possible.

I've been pitching in front of a camera for many years, generating more than $2 billion in revenue from it, so it's fair to say that I know a lot about the craft, the process and what works best to get the results you want. In this chapter, I'm going to share a few of my key points of success in video marketing: I'm going to explain "The 5 E's" I use to make sure my pitches in front of a camera generate the highest ROI possible.

Engage

The first "E" is one of the most important things you must do with any form of marketing: get the people's attention! To do that, you have to engage them immediately.

A great way to do that is to present a problem and put in the form of a question. Are you overweight and can't shake those extra pounds? Having trouble sleeping, and can't find relief? Are there stains in your clothes that you just can't get rid of? When you ask those kinds of instant-impact questions, you immediately engage the interest of anyone who has that particular problem, and, of course, you're setting yourself up anticipation with your audience as they now expect you to be the person who has the solution.

Video also has the great advantage of giving you the opportunity to visually bring that problem to life. Think about the commercial where they pour red wine on a white carpet. A viewer's immediate reaction is: *They're never going to get that stain out.* But you still stay tuned to see how they do it!

Lastly, make sure you're presenting the viewer with a problem that's very, very common to the niche group you're targeting. In the early days of pitching on television, an advertiser, of course, had to present a problem that was as universal to a broad audience as possible to appeal to as many of the millions and millions who were watching. The internet has changed the game so that you can now cost-effectively target a very specific crowd that has a very specific problem with your amazing solution. You just have to make sure it's a problem that really hits home with that target group and that you have a compelling solution to offer.

Enroll

What do I mean by "enroll?" I mean, you want to get viewers on board with your message and make them feel a part of what you're pitching. You do that first by making viewers feel on equal footing with you. Never talk down to them, and avoid negative wording in your script. And just as importantly, make your pitch about *them*, and not you. Empathize, relate and mirror their values, needs and desires to demonstrate that you are right there with them, and you're guiding them to a great solution!

One of the big issues that people have when they get in front of a camera is that they immediately try to establish their credibility by talking about how wonderful they are. Wrong approach. The truth is, the word you should be using the most in any video is "you," as in, "I'm here to help *you*," "Because I'm an expert in so-and-so, it will make a difference to *you*," or "Because I went through this difficult time, I know how this problem can affect *you*." If you can't relate whatever you say about yourself directly to the viewer's needs and wants, you might as well keep quiet about it.

Another way you enroll people is by *showing your own personal vulnerability*. I know this book is about us being "superheroes" in marketing, but you have to remember that superheroes always have a *flaw*. Viewers don't want to see a superhero without a weakness. That's boring, flat, and we can't relate to that kind of person. That's why Superman has Kryptonite, Iron Man has a self-destructive ego and the Hulk has, well, kind of a bad attitude. As marketers, we also have to be unafraid to show our flaws. Even master motivator Tony Robbins, who looks absolutely perfect, is quick to tell his crowd that he started life in a 400-square-foot apartment, only had Ramen Noodles to eat and had to work as a janitor to make ends meet. Superheroes overcome adversity, rise above challenges and work to make the world a better place for all because of it.

To make yourself *human* is a powerful enrolling quality, and the best way to do that is to present your own personal struggle to your audience. If you're a rich kid born with a silver spoon in your mouth and life was easy from birth, we don't believe we can learn anything from that experience. We identify with the underdogs, the struggles and fights, and we want to find out how *they* made good—how they changed things for the better.

Empower

The next "E" is all about improving your viewers' lives. When you enroll them, they believe you can help them climb a ladder. When you then choose to empower them, you're showing them *how* to climb that ladder, and your product should be making it easy for them to do it.

One way you can empower is through the use of testimonials, either verbal ones, visual ones, or ones given through social proof. You begin by revealing how you overcame a challenge and then show the viewer three other people who did it telling their stories. There are different kinds of people you can feature in these testimonials: a real person, a celebrity or an expert, such as a doctor, telling you why a certain product is the best one to buy.

A healthy combination of all those different testimonials is, to me, one of the keys to success, depending on what your product is. For a skin care product, I want to see a real person, a doctor and a clinical trial. For a shampoo that cleans my carpet or a pet product, the stakes aren't quite as high—you just need to show buyers who loved what the product did for them.

Empowerment should be a basic part of your pitch. What do I mean by that? Let's say I ask you what you do and you answer, "Well, I'm a video producer." That answer just makes me start to yawn, because the cold, cold truth is that I don't care what you do. I care about *what you can do for me*. So, switch your focus from yourself to empowering *them*. It's not that hard to do – it's just a matter of changing your answer with a different focus in mind. For that video producer, the response should be something like, "Forbes, you know what I do? I help entrepreneurs live their dreams. Most of them struggle to find an amazing and impactful way to market their product – so I help them create videos that sell and sell big, and I can do it for virtually any product."

Now you have my attention!

Entertain

This "E" can be boiled down to three very important words: *Don't Be Boring.*

There's a reason they put the word "Show" in front of "Business." It's because you need to entertain people with your pitch, and this is doubly true with a video. Think about the most memorable infomercial moments that come to mind, like Vince selling ShamWow, looking at the audience and saying, "Hey, Camera Guy, come here!" Or Judith Light doing her first Proactiv spot and crying on camera about how painful her acne was. Entertaining? You bet, but in a whole different way, because it's emotionally involving and cathartic (and, by the way, Proactiv is now a billion-dollar company). They entertained their audience by giving them a reason to pay attention, care and remember.

Even though it sounds counter-intuitive, *education* can even be entertaining, although it did lead to a few very stressful on-camera moments for me. I once sold an insole product on a home shopping channel. Now, generally, you get ten to fifteen minutes to sell a product, and you're supposed to generate between two to three thousand dollars per minute as you're doing it. Well, what I did to show how this gel insole product helps your feet was to get the foot of a skeleton and a whole tub of sand, and talk about how, when your foot gets in sand, it has to move and groove. When a doctor puts your foot in a hard cast, however, the muscles atrophy because they don't get worked. The gel product acts like sand, making your foot work in all the right ways.

That's a pretty long explanation, and, as I was halfway through it, all the guys in the control room started freaking out. The reason? I wasn't bringing in two or three thousand bucks every 60 seconds - nope, I was making ZERO sales. But that was happening only because viewers were too engrossed in my "lecture" to call and order the product! A few minutes later, however, the phones started ringing and we started doing $10,000 a minute in sales.

That's entertainment!

Education is important when you're pitching a product that's a whole new concept. And again, don't talk down to your audience, keep it on an educated sixth-grader level and speak with your viewers in their language. Don't use the kind of ten-dollar words that a college professor might throw around, and whatever you do, stay away from industry jargon! Unless you're selling only within your own industry, you will alienate everyone else listening to you. Also, try to teach and entertain quickly and visually with animation, pictures or props.

Finally, keep in mind people have a greatly diminished attention span these days. Some marketers say to me, "Forbes, I saved my best stuff for the end of the video." My response? "Nobody *watches* the end of the video!" It's true. Your audience will not wait. Grab them at the beginning the best way you can. Journalists are taught to always give the most important stuff up at the beginning of an article, then they add in the details for those interested enough to get a more in-depth reporting. Literally, the content that matters most and that's the most exciting starts the script, then the next important information comes next and so forth, until you've completed your whole pitch. But, you must grab them first to even have a chance at taking them through to the end of your video. Don't hold back!

My final point, when it comes to entertaining, is that you must learn to be an expert storyteller. Make sure your video has a very clear beginning, middle and end. If you don't, you will not make sales. At some point, you actually have to close, and if you don't build your marketing pitch to the right high point, that won't happen.

Enlighten

When you *enlighten* your viewers, you're showing them something that takes things to a whole new level. Show them a product that's innovative and interesting in some way they've never seen before. Which brings me to one of my secret superhero marketing tips: You don't need to create an entirely new product from scratch for it to sell well through a video. To have a best-selling product, you just need to improve on the story and pitch of what's already out there. In other words, your mission is to build a better mousetrap in whatever product category you're dabbling in. For example, the latest models of smartphones are in no way, shape or form reinventions. They're simply improved in one way or another. And yet, people still line up around the block when the new iPhone is released, right?

Almost every superhero has some kind of weapon or unique power, and mine is the SpinGym®, which I sell through my own company. It's my "better mousetrap" and the perfect example of what I'm talking about, because SpinGym® is a simple portable fitness system that's unlike anything else out there. It's only three pieces of metal strung together with a cord, and yet I've sold almost two million of these things, because it's designed to make your arms sexy and strong!

I'll let you in on something: the first time I wanted to sell it on television, I was told to go home, that it wouldn't work. But, I had unshakable faith in it. Not only that, but I knew how to pitch it on camera. One of the keys was that I had great visuals to show how it really toned up muscles, and that kind of live demonstration is just the kind of thing that will enlighten viewers, because it actually *shows* them why it's different, why it's exciting and that it *works*.

But people thought I was crazy, because the SpinGym® is actually a kind of yo-yo. It's a re-working of a 2000-year-old Chinese toy. When they first looked at it, nobody thought it could be an exercise product of any value. But then again, a jump rope was just a piece of rope lying on the floor. A kettle bell was just a hunk of metal with no apparent use. The point is, it's not what it is, it's what you do with it. I had a clear vision of how to sell the SpinGym® in such a way that it would *enlighten* people and show them how to use this "toy" so that it was clear how it improved the way they looked and felt.

So... how are you enlightening your audience with what you're selling? Do you know? You should, and then create a business plan and a clear vision around that enlightenment.

Excite

Finally, I want to leave you with a bonus "E" – **Excite.** I come at everything with a tremendous amount of energy and passion. I want you to LOVE what I have to show you when you see it on television. I want you to get so excited that you have to have it *now.* That element of excitement seeps into the video you produce, and your audience gets excited with you—they literally can feel your energy and enthusiasm.

So get pumped about your video, put that level of excitement, passion and commitment into it, and make sure you're doing everything possible to Engage, Enroll, Empower, Entertain and Enlighten your target group through your video pitch! That's the only way you enjoy Excellent results.

Animate Your Marketing Conversation

Creating Videos that Stand Out and Increase Your Sales in 60 Seconds (Or Less!)

By Byron G. Torres

Creativity plays a huge part in making marketing memorable – but too often, we focus on the technological mechanics at the expense of creating an entertaining and eye-catching message.

That's where a guy like Byron G.Torres comes in handy. Byron's passionate about creating marketing videos that stand out because of his not-so-secret ingredient, high-quality animation. Find out more about this Marketing Avenger's distinctive storytelling "weapon of choice" in this informative and illuminating chapter.

- Richard Seppala

THINK ABOUT THE PERSON you'd like to watch your latest marketing video, a video you slaved over and are counting on to deliver great results to your company.

Now think about how, when that person first sees your video pop up in their Facebook newsfeed, his smartphone might signal an incoming text. Or a notification from his sports app suddenly reveals his team has just scored in a big game. Maybe, in the background, his office TV starts blaring about a breaking news event. And all of this is happening while he's trying to get a project done by a brutal deadline.

Let's face it, this isn't an abnormal situation – everybody's life is incredibly time-challenged these days. And with all that going on, do you think this potential customer – or any potential customer – is going to pay attention to a marketing video that fails to command his attention?

That's just today's reality. As any Marketing Avenger will tell you, there's a lot of noise out there, noise that stands a good chance at drowning out your message, no matter how many platforms you use to send it out. That's why, more than ever, you need a dramatic difference in your marketing creative approach.

Animation is one of the best ways to make that difference.

Animation naturally grabs a viewer's attention, whether they're scrolling through their Facebook newsfeed or fast forwarding through a show on their DVR. Animation makes your target group stop, look – and, most importantly, *listen* - to your message.

And that's why I bet on animation to make my clients look good and sell hard. It's a bet that continues to pay off.

Banking on a New Direction

I believe you really have to be passionate about what you do in life.

About ten years ago, I wasn't so passionate about my job. I was working in the banking industry, making six figures a year, which was nice – but what wasn't so nice was the fact that I was feeling completely bored about what I was doing. What I really wanted to do was be *creative* – something banks aren't exactly known for.

So, in 2007, I took a leap of faith and started Pritzer Media. No, my new company wasn't based in a fancy office in a posh downtown high-rise. The truth is, I started it in the loft of my home. At the beginning, all I did was sell media time to my clients, which still wasn't the most exciting thing in the world – but at least I was running my own business and not working for somebody else.

Then one day, a client asked me if I did website design. I said no, I didn't. Then another client asked me the same thing. Again, I said no. When the third guy showed up to ask me the same question, I realized that the answer I should have been giving all along was, "Yes, what do you need?" And that's what I said the third time around. I figured out how to deliver this new service, I got to exercise a few creative muscles, and my business began to expand.

Over the next few years, I kept adding marketing services I could offer to my clients – in fact, I added so many that, by the time the end of 2013 rolled around, I thought it was necessary to produce a video showing everything Pritzer Media now had to offer. And I decided the best way to do that was with animation. I hired an animator to do the job mostly on his own – but when I took a look at it, I saw it didn't work. It was pretty, but it didn't tell the right story and it didn't do a good job of *selling* us. So I decided to go in and work directly with the animator to produce the kind of result I wanted. Okay, maybe I drove him up the wall - but I knew what I wanted the piece to be and wanted to make sure that's how it turned out. When I was done, I was excited – the video came out even better than I thought it would.

And that made me think another step ahead.

As I watched the finished video, I thought to myself that this was exactly the kind of thing that one of my existing clients needed to implement in his current marketing campaign.

I reached out to him, we got together and I showed him the animated video. And I said, "Hey, we need to do this for you, let's talk about it." And that's how that initial video that I made strictly as a promotional piece for my own company ended up making me $30,000 in two weeks. The video that was supposed to be my calling card for my existing business turned out to be a calling card for a whole *new* business, which I named "Vid Machine." (vidmachine.com). I discovered that animation was something I loved to do that could also generate a lot of revenue. My creative juices were flowing and my business instincts were tingling.

Where was the downside? I couldn't see any.

So I jumped in with both feet. I put together a creative team of storytellers and animators to work in house because I believed we would get better results for our clients if we fed off one another's creativity and synergy. Financially, outsourcing this kind of work to India or the Philippines definitely made more sense – but creatively? No. To me, my creative input and marketing background made the first video work well enough to get me another. That situation would be hard to duplicate if the animators were halfway around the world. I didn't want to scrimp on the creative effort in any aspect.

So I didn't.

The result so far: Our videos have helped generate tens of millions of dollars in sales for ourselves and for our clients.

Our Number One Priority: Increase Sales for Our Clients

As time goes on and we evolve with the market, Vid Machine continues to generate more exciting results with each video we produce. We make sure our videos sell our clients' services and products, making our videos highly effective as well as entertaining. When writing and producing each video, we make sure that the format and message will allow our clients to use them on TV, on social media sites, on websites, wherever they can make their impact. And we make sure that impact is as big as possible.

At the beginning of this chapter, I talked about all the noise all of us Marketing Avengers have to battle on an everyday basis – that noise is a tough villain to vanquish! Well, animation can be the decisive factor in whether someone watches your video or moves on to something else without a second thought. When they see a video is animated, and that the animation is telling a story in such a way that it captures their attention and doesn't let it go, the ROI can be amazing.

Of course, there's more to making a great marketing video than animation alone. We're not making funny cartoons that have no purpose. No, what separates us from other animation companies is that, first and foremost, we have a *marketing and sales mindset* in place.

Why is that important? Because it's easy to get carried away with yourself and think you're making the most amazing piece of art in the world. And maybe you are – but the real question is, are you serving the needs of your client? Pretty pictures aren't enough – and your real objective with animation, or any other kind of marketing media for that matter, is to *sell* something. The marketing video has to be short and to the point to make sure it is assisting in the sale. "What do you do and how can you help me?" is all a potential customer is thinking. A well-produced sales/marketing video has to answer that question by delivering your message clearly – which, in turn, will help increase your sales in 60 seconds or less! That end goal has to be inside the creators' heads during the entirety of production and we never forget that.

The Amazing Attraction of Animation

Why does animation produce higher ROI results when compared to other types of videos?

There are several reasons, but one big one is the simple fact that almost every one of us *grew up watching cartoons*. There's still a pleasure center packed into our memories that gets activated when we see animation – and immediately attracts us to that kind of content. Something in our brain shouts, "I want to watch this!"

That doesn't happen with most so-called "marketing" videos, which frequently feature talking heads or a spokesperson discussing benefits of a product. Viewers immediately process those kinds of videos as being "just another commercial" – and that immediately turns off a lot of people, because they're used to doing everything possible to *avoid* watching commercials. Why watch another one – unless it's selling something the viewer has a specific interest in?

With animation, you can sneak your message past the mental gatekeepers in your potential customers' heads. The animation is colorful and fun, it's eye candy instead of an everyday advertisement. And yet, we still make sure the marketing message is still in there and strong - as long as we can grab their attention, we can pull them through to whatever Call to Action we place within the video.

Animation establishes credibility without looking like it's a hard sell that viewers have to endure. It gives some value back to the viewer simply by being animated; the animation shows that the company cares enough to put some extra money behind creating a fun video that's enjoyable to watch. Even if the animation is done as an overlay over live-action footage, it's still a great enhancement.

As Mary Poppins once sang, "A spoonful of sugar makes the medicine go down." Converting that lyric for my own purposes, you could also say, "A minute of animation makes the marketing a whole lot sweeter."

(Oh, and let's also not forget that what made *Mary Poppins* such a hit was the addition of animation!)

The Advantages of Animation

Animation also has a very distinct edge when it comes to dealing with a product or service that has incredible benefits that might be a tad difficult to explain.

For example, we have a number of clients with online platforms that are difficult to explain. That's okay – because, if during our initial meeting it takes them a few minutes to describe what they do, I know we're going to be a great fit in helping them.

And that's not by creating a long-winded boring lecture-style video that most people won't stay awake through. It makes more sense to break down each element into shorter easy-to-follow videos - and then produce one main marketing video that quickly and effectively explains the solution and benefits that the service delivers. The end result...increased sales.

Animation helps make a complex idea simple and allows you to speak one-on-one to the viewer in a way that doesn't get bogged down in the technical details. Result? To date, millions of dollars in sales generated for our clients using the videos we've produced for them.

The Value of Originality

I can't stress enough the value of producing original animation, as opposed to the cookie-cutter whiteboard videos you can have automatically made on some websites. Those are fine for certain things, but they generally don't deliver the kind of results most marketers are after, because they lack the kind of creative spark that makes great animated videos really shine – and deliver tons of conversions.

That's why you should work with a dedicated top-level creative team that has a grip on marketing basics. Some animators are great at plying their craft on computers, but have no concept of what needs to be done to make the actual sale. If they don't have the right guidance, they may deliver an absolutely beautiful piece of work – that may absolutely deliver you little to no result.

Length is another important issue. If you put a three or four-minute video out there, it almost doesn't matter how good it is, because virtually nobody is going to watch it. You want to deliver your message in under sixty seconds for maximum effect. There are exceptions to that rule, but whenever a client comes in and asks me to do a three-minute video, I tell them, "If I can make your video work in under a minute, you should pay me the price of a three-minute video – because I took something that wasn't going to make you any money into something that will."

Let me make one more point about marketing with animation: The content cannot suck. I say that jokingly – but I'm also serious. Animation is a technique that can't make up for a lame concept or weak messaging. You have to make your content so valuable that people are not only going to want to watch it themselves – but also share it with everybody they know. When you can hit that sweet spot, the video takes on a life of its own and it becomes a part of your sales force, increasing revenue and profits.

The unlimited possibilities of animation in marketing excite me to no end. I get so pumped up when I'm talking to my clients about a project that they catch the fever too.

That's why I'm looking for every way possible to do everything I can with animation. Animation is able to take something that doesn't exist – and make it tangible on the screen. You can create whatever you want and you're able to tell a story in such a way that people are going to want to watch it over and over again.

XYes, noise is everywhere, always threatening to drown out your message. Animation? It's perceived as a *respite* from the noise. It makes people feel good and, in turn, makes them *want* to hear what you have to say. So put animation to work for your product or service. You can bet on an *animated* response in return.

The Ultimate "Shock and Awe" Marketing Weapon

Destroys Competition & Turns You into a Victorious Superhero!

By Devin A. Herz

With over two decades of marketing experience under his belt, Devin Herz, Founder and Chief Creative Consultant of DMC (Dynamic Marketing Consultants), is no stranger to super-heroics – especially when it comes to helping business owners and entrepreneurs promote and sell their products and services all the way from Main Street to Wall Street.

One big reason for his long-term success is that he doesn't let any grass grow under his feet - he's constantly on the lookout for new and exciting ways to make his clients stand out from the crowd.

And you're about to find out about one of his biggest and best marketing innovations in this very chapter!

- Richard Seppala

THOR HAS HIS HAMMER. Captain America has his shield. Spider-Man has his webbing. And the Green Arrow has...well, his arrows.

Most superheroes have their signature weapon – the thing that allows them to triumph again and again when they do battle. It also becomes their trademark; the item that makes them memorable and allows them to stand out from the other costumed crusaders.

Like the superheroes, any business also needs a primary marketing "weapon" to make its mark. And that weapon needs to be as accurate as the Captain's shield, as all-powerful as Thor's hammer – and it also needs to remain in the intended audience's mind, just as strongly as Spidey's web sticks to walls.

Our marketing company, Dynamic Marketing Consultants (or DMC for short), discovered such a weapon, and it has resulted in an incredible number of success stories for our clients - including actually getting a law passed in New York City!

So read on and find out about an amazing marketing and sales solution that doesn't require any reading... because you *watch* it instead.

On the Cutting Edge with PrintAVizion, a.k.a. Video-In-Print

As marketers, our job is to stay ahead of the curve. Our mantra for our clients is to "use the kind of marketing that your competition hasn't even heard of yet." So, over the years, we've focused a great deal on unique forms of direct marketing in an attempt to always keep our clients ahead of their competition.

We began researching this particular technology an entire decade ago. Back then, it was so new (and so expensive) that it simply wasn't cost-efficient for most of our clients. But we knew it was a winner – and that it was just a matter of time before the technology would catch up. So we made sure to keep tabs on it.

Finally, about five years ago, we discovered the price had come down far enough that we could make it work. And because we had been relentless in keeping track of this exciting innovation, we were pumped to realize we would be among the first companies in the world to offer this technology to our clients as a marketing tool.

PrintAVizion soon became one of our client's most incredible marketing weapons.

The Video-In-Print technology is pretty self-descriptive: packaged as what seems to be a small hardback book or brochure, the recipient opens it to instead discover (to their awe and delight) a paper-thin LCD video screen embedded right there in the print page. The surrounding packaging may contain text or photos, as well. But the most intriguing aspect is certainly the video-within-the-book.

These Video Books and Video Brochures are completely rechargeable so your user can view your videos over and over again, allowing them to show it to their friends and business associates. And what's more, we've seen that as the price of Video-In-Print technology keeps coming down, the quality of the videos just keeps getting better.

Frankly, it's an amazing solution – the visual impact immediately captivates the recipient, who can actually *see* and hear your message, rather than just reading it.

Now, you might think it would be easier to load up an iPad or similar tablet with a video and get the same results. However, those tablets do a multitude of things – which means your video can easily get lost in the shuffle. With our PrintAVizion solution, it's all about – and it's *only* about – your marketing video, your commercial, your sales pitch, your gallery of products and services, your glowing testimonials... whatever content you want to feature on the actual video, which, by the way, will play with full, great-quality sound and picture – no compromise!

And, like a real book, a Video Book can have different "chapters" or video messages. For instance, your Video Book might have four buttons inside which, when pressed, allows the "readers" to skip to four different "chapters." One button could take them to a video introduction from you, another could feature some of your services, a third might show them some testimonials, and the fourth could feature a call to action.

All of these customizable features offer you complete control over your message and its delivery – packaged in such a unique (and dare I say, *cool*) way that people are sure to show it off to their business associates, family, and friends.

PrintAVizion can also be used for catalogs, sales, new member welcome kits, whale prospects, program overviews, testimonial showcases, and anything else you can imagine. The potential for your video message is limited only by your creativity.

How about even having a catalog that has a custom video for each page? If you want to have multiple pages in your PrintAVizion catalog, it's now possible to have a cut-out window on each page. Every time someone turns one of the pages, the video skips ahead to the appropriate video for that page. For example, if the book you're reading now were a Video Book, you could turn the page to Richard's chapter and his video would begin playing - then you could turn the page to my chapter and suddenly my video would start playing.

Obviously, there are less expensive ways to send video messages. You could simply send a DVD with your video on it. But how many people will take the time to unwrap the DVD, insert it in the DVD player, and sit down to watch it - especially in this day and age of insanely-convenient streaming? I mean, I know a lot of people who don't even own a DVD player anymore. In contrast, think about how many *more* will watch what's inside a PrintAVizion product – simply because all they have to do is open it and take a look at what they're already holding in their hands? Not to mention the fact that it is very likely to be the first Video-In-Print piece they've ever seen, the novelty alone is guaranteed to intrigue them!

Is PrintAVizion for You?

PrintAVizion has turned out to be one of the most amazing high-end prospecting and sales tools that we have to offer. However, they are best for clients who will get a good ROI out of each individual purchase.

Obviously, PrintAVizion won't be cost-effective for somebody selling six dollar cheeseburgers. But the manufacturer who's selling $5000 systems or packages? The consultant who's after long-term contracts? A dentist selling dental implants for which a patient might spend $30,000? These are ideal candidates.

Here are just a few ways in which our clients have used the PrintAVizion technology:

- Welcome Kits
- Shock & Awe Mailers
- Sales Tools
- Point of Purchase Displays
- Specialty Packaging
- Training Manuals
- Education
- Video Direct Mail
- Print Collateral
- Magazine Inserts
- Catalogs
- Keepsakes

Of course the cost of producing PrintAVizion can be an understandable concern, but it's important to consider the huge benefits they can deliver. If you stand to make a thousand dollars on a sale, is it worth the investment of fifty or a hundred dollars to make that happen? The savvy business owner would say it is.

To illustrate, realtors specializing in high-end properties find the PrintAVizion Video Books to be a great marketing tool when used to impress potential clients. The book can describe the agent's services and show testimonials from other satisfied clients who were happy with the way this agent handled their real estate transactions. It immediately shows the prospective client you are cutting-edge and that you will take a unique marketing approach to selling their home. It can also show photos or video of the high-end properties recently listed or sold by the agent. The book can be tailored to the price ranges and tastes of the agent's preferred clientele and will surely capture the potential clients' undivided attention.

PrintAVizion also offers great sales opportunities to the higher education market. Colorado State University uses them to motivate students to enroll in courses where the subject matter may not easily be explained in the course listing. It's a great way to illustrate what some courses teach in an exciting, visual way, motivating more potential students to sign up for those courses. End result: more profits for the school.

Let's talk about consultants, coaches and other entrepreneurs who traditionally sell their own information products through, say, a 12-CD or DVD set. How much easier is it for one of their clients to get the same information through two hours of content in a Video Book? They can just pick it up and resume watching it whenever they want!

Here are a few more examples of what our clients have done with PrintAVizion:

- Allstate's corporate recruiters used Video Books to convert insurance agents who owned their own agencies.

- Professional speakers marketing their availability for speaking engagements included their sizzle reels and snippets of speeches to demonstrate their impact to potential audiences at upcoming events.

- Xenex sent out one thousand Video Books to hospital administrators to demonstrate their new germ-zapping robots – the latest technology for fighting contagious threats such as an Ebola outbreak.

- Attorneys, dentists, and other professional practice owners have used PrintAVizion to educate and inform their clients. Lawyers, for example, used Video Books to inform their clients on what they can expect to experience during a case, whether it's a divorce, bankruptcy, malpractice, or any other kind. Dentists, similarly, used the devices to educate their patients on certain treatments in which they may be interested.

• Billionaire Mark Cuban used Video Books to sell season tickets and private suite seating for professional sporting events at the American Airlines Center sports arena in Dallas. (If Mark Cuban takes a personal interest in using your marketing tool, you know it has to be a winner.)

As this chapter's title indicates, I believe that PrintAVizion has the ability to create the ultimate "shock and awe" vibe because this technology doesn't necessarily have to be delivered in the form of a book. It can be integrated into a box containing all your marketing materials which, when opened, will instantly play a video featuring you greeting the recipients and explaining the contents of the package. *It's a live sales presentation in a box!* These videos can also be mounted on postcard-sized materials that can be sent out in simple mailing envelopes – or even on business cards, believe it or not, if you really want to make a splash. Think of what an impact those marketing tools could have on your next campaign!

However you want to use the concept, there's no question that the Video Book can be incredibly influential.

Remember when I mentioned earlier how a Video Book actually got legislation passed? It's true. In an effort to avoid the local taxes and license fees on their cars, New York residents had begun registering them in nearby Philadelphia, Pennsylvania. Since opponents of this tax dodge feared that the issue might be a well-kept secret from some lawmakers, they distributed Video Books describing the problem to lawmakers in New York City as they entered the state house to consider the vote on a new law banning automobile registrations in another state.

As you can imagine, the bill passed.

Your Overall Marketing Strategy

It's important to note that, as with any marketing "weapon," PrintAVizion needs to be part of an organization's overall marketing strategy. And that strategy can be tough to create from within the organization. First, it's expensive to maintain the type of in-house marketing expertise you need to promote your company correctly. Second, you invariably are too close to what you're trying to sell— you lose objectivity and, with that objectivity gone, you easily lose sight of what the right marketing approach might be for your business. Finally, most business owners are simply too busy running their companies to devote the time necessary to develop effective marketing plans. And that can be costly in terms of lost sales and opportunities.

That's where my company, DMC, can really be YOUR advantage above the competition. With our Marketing Mastery system, we analyze your current business position along with your future business goals and prepare a marketing plan to help you achieve—and hopefully surpass—your goals. We can then implement those plans, providing your business with a team of specialists who work virtually to fulfill all your marketing needs at the highest possible level.

While the creation of a long-term marketing plan seems like an obvious method for business success, a surprising number of businesses fail to put such a plan in place. Many simply throw a handful of different messages into the marketplace, hoping something hits the bullseye. Occasionally, we see this strategy used even by successful businesses, and we wonder how much more business they might gain if they actually implemented an integrated, comprehensive plan.

From a personal standpoint, I see this often, as I can't help but analyze everyone's marketing efforts—it's in my blood! My dad owned retail stores in the New Jersey area, and, from a young age, I was very interested in helping out with his marketing design and advertising. As a teenager, I even got to compose some ads on my own. All of that early training quickly taught me what worked and what didn't—and also inspired me to make marketing my career. Early on, I was lucky to have the professional opportunity to work with the New York Yankees, where I learned what it takes to make a winning organization, and the importance of communicating that positive image to the public. My experience taught me about the success that can come from creating unique marketing that's memorable and impactful.

At DMC, we strive to get our clients noticed in a way that makes them look good—and causes people to see them in the best possible light. To do that, we go the extra mile to understand who their customers and clients are, what they look for in a business, and, most importantly, what motivates them to buy.

PrintAVizion is just one example of our quest to find new and innovative marketing solutions that no one else has tried before; solutions that extend all the way from traditional direct mail to the latest cutting-edge online marketing opportunities.

If you want to see how PrintAVizion might work for your company – or if you'd like to explore any other unique and powerful marketing solutions – I'd be excited to talk to you.

As I said at the beginning, a signature "weapon" can make anyone into a superhero – and we'd love to help you find the one that will shoot you into the stratosphere!

M.

The Online Dynamic Duo: Retargeting and Real Time Bidding

By Todd McPartlin and Chris Ormiston

Online marketing is becoming more sophisticated by the day – and many businesses just don't know how to keep up and reap all the benefits available from it. Staying on the cutting edge of online marketing requires a huge commitment of time and energy - according to SmartInsights.com, most marketers spend 60% of their time on digital marketing these days. But what choice is there? If you don't stay current, you get left behind by your competition.

Enter Todd McPartlin and Chris Ormiston, two guys that take this massive burden off many a marketer's back. They not only help their clients market to already-interested leads efficiently and effectively, they also help them get out in front of potential customers that don't know what those clients have to offer – but just might buy from them if they did. In this chapter, you'll find out about two of this tremendous twosome's most powerful online marketing tactics – and just how much value they can add to your brand.

- Richard Seppala

WHEN IT COMES TO SELLING ONLINE, businesses have two immediate needs: (1) identifying new leads that would be interested in what they have to offer and (2) continuing to market to leads that are already aware of them but have yet to make a purchase.

In this chapter, we're going to talk about two major marketing tactics that answer each of those needs, retargeting and RTB (Real Time Bidding). If you're unaware of what retargeting and RTB are and the massive benefits they can deliver to your business, then you definitely need to read on and learn more. Yes, sometimes all this internet jargon can make your eyes glaze over, but we're going to explain both of these in terms you'll not only understand, but will also enable you to see just how powerful both these concepts are – not to mention how much value they can deliver to any business that leverages them to its benefit.

So, without further ado, let's find out more about the Dynamic Duo of retargeting and RTB.

What is Retargeting?

For those of you who don't know what retargeting is all about, it's a pretty simple concept. Let's say someone visits a business website, but they end up just looking around and leaving. They don't sign up for emails, they don't buy, they don't actively pursue any kind of engagement with the business. However, the business itself is still able to keep track of the lead through cookies, pixel tracking and so forth. Through retargeting, when the lead continues using a browser to view other websites, the business is able to keep marketing to them through online ads that follow the lead around and remind them to come back to the site, perhaps even offer a deal if they do.

What's the point of retargeting? Why is it important? Well, the answer to both questions is simple: *You don't want to lose a potential customer.* And that's all too easy to do if you only rely on your website to sell your products and/or services.

What you have to remember is *98 percent of visitors to your website leave without doing anything.* Now, if you had a brick-and-mortar store, would you let 98 percent of the people wandering in just wander right back out without at least asking if you can help them? Of course not. That's why you need to look at retargeting as the virtual equivalent of a salesperson asking a customer if they need anything.

What you also have to remember is you may be doing the lead a *favor* by retargeting them. They may have come to your website intending to take action and got sidetracked instead. We all know how easy it is to get distracted when we're online. A Facebook update comes in, an email shows up, there are a thousand things that can take you away from what you're doing and cause you to forget to finish something you fully intended to follow through on. By reminding the lead they were at your website, you're often offering a helpful service – which is why such a high percentage of consumers actually *like* retargeting.

Studies show that over 30 percent of consumers have either a positive or very positive reaction to retargeted ads – and only 11 percent have a negative reaction. The greatest percentage, 59 percent, don't really care one way or the other – so you have very little to lose with retargeting and an incredible amount to gain.

One more important note about retargeting: If you're not doing it, your competition likely is. One in five marketers now has a dedicated budget for retargeting, in addition to those who just make it happen out of their general marketing funds.

Why Every Business Needs Retargeting

There's a reason why companies like Kimberly-Clark, the packaged goods powerhouse, relies on retargeting. For its part, the corporation says the tactic delivers 50 to 60 percent higher conversion rates among consumers.

Retargeting is all about delivering the right message to the right consumer at the right moment. The lead is already in a mindset of wanting what you have to sell – otherwise, they never would have visited your website to begin with. It just makes sense to hit them again with ads when they're still in that mindset and they hopefully haven't made a purchase from someone else yet.

Retargeting also boosts the ROI for all forms of marketing. The statistics on its success are truly mind-blowing – here are just a few of the proven numbers.

- Retargeting can boost ad response up to 400%.
- Retargeted customers are 4x times more likely to convert than new customers.
- Retargeted ads lead to a +1046% increase in branded search.
- Web visitors who have been retargeted with display ads are 70% more likely to convert
- Websites see a 726% lift in site visitation after 4 weeks of re-targeting exposure
- 72% of online shoppers are likely to abandon their carts before checking out. Without retargeting, *only 8% of those customers* return to complete their transaction.
- The average click-through rate for display ads is 0.07 percent. The average click-through for retargeted ads? About 0.7 percent.

Not only that, but retargeting is also ideal for either upselling or cross-selling to a different (but related) product or service. Being drawn to products in advertisements is the most commonly noted reason consumers gave for clicking on a retargeted ad (37 percent). Consumers also said retargeted ads are a convenient way to visit a website they already intended to visit (28 percent) and for desiring more information on the product in the ad (21 percent).

And quite frankly, there's a lot of value to retargeting simply for branding purposes. The companies that do retargeting look bigger and more professional when their ads start showing up on popular and influential websites such as WebMD and CNN.com. It's a very low cost way to look like a big player – as well as to boost your conversions and your bottom line.

Again, more and more marketers are dedicating more and more resources to their retargeting efforts, due to the tactic's extreme effectiveness. Over 90 percent of marketers say that retargeted ads are as good as or better than what has been the gold standard in digital marketing, search ads, according to a recent survey by leading retargeter, AdRoll. Adam Berke, CMO and President of AdRoll, says the reason for retargeting's value is consumer intent. In his words, "When you combine this hyper-valuable data set with advanced media buying technology, algorithmic bidding, dynamic creative, and reach across publishers and channels, you end up with an extremely important marketing channel that is now viewed to be as crucial as search engine marketing."

What is RTB?

Now, let's turn to the second member of this chapter's Dynamic Duo – another online marketing tactic which perfectly complements retargeting.

RTB, Real Time Bidding, uses the exact same technology as is used for retargeting – but instead of chasing after consumers that have already been on your site, it allows you to get in front of ideal prospects *before* they've visited it. In other words, it's a tactic to *drive* desirable traffic your way – after which you can then retarget them and follow them around as we just described.

Here's how it works. Imagine McDonalds and Pepsi both want to have their ads appear on a web page that appeals to a certain niche of consumer. There is space at the top of the web page for an ad and also at the bottom and the top position is preferable.

Now, let's say McDonalds bids $1.50 to have their ad show to a thousand people in the top spot (that's what we call CPM, Cost Per Thousand). And let's say Pepsi is bidding $1.20. Neither company knows what the other is bidding, their bids have already been entered and this entire process suddenly happens in a few milliseconds. The result, in this case, is that McDonalds wins the top ad – it shows up at the cost of $1.50. Pepsi gets the bottom ad at the cost of $1.20.

RTB is to digital advertising what high-frequency trading is to Wall Street. It involves computerized, algorithm-driven trading that allows for quick buying of ad impressions according to pre-set parameters. Instead of booking advertising space in advance, blindly betting on what will be effective at the time your online ad actually appears, you are instead dealing with what's most effective and most affordable *at the moment the ad will appear* – so that you can instantly take advantage of the best advertising deals and the best placements for your particular brand that are available at the time.

The Benefits of RTB

Now – why does your business want to use RTB?

Well, first of all, it's usually less expensive than other forms of paid search. Other marketing platforms that offer the same kind of online exposure such as Facebook and PPC can get very expensive for certain niches. RTB can deliver the same high-level results, but at a much cheaper price, making it a very affordable and powerful tactic.

Another important advantage RTB has over other direct response marketing such as direct mail and PPC is that RTB is infinitely more flexible and targeted. With other systems, you're paying a flat rate or bid in advance and you're locked into your choices. With RTB, you're bidding on online display ad inventory on the fly and you're able to change up content and audience targeting as you go along.

That in turn means you're also able to continually optimize your online campaigns by testing simultaneous marketing strategies. Instead of taking hours or even days to change up ads that aren't working, you can rapidly test, change and retest in real-time – and instantly see what kind of ad content will improve response rates and change up your strategy to emphasis that content. While your audience is still engaged, you can increase click-through rates, engagement rates and reach by simple trial and error.

You can also drill down on sites right down to a very specific geolocation, which is, of course, very critical for a local marketer. A dentist, for example, will probably not want to target an entire metro area – some distances will simply be too far for potential patients, they won't want to travel that long for dental appointments on a regular basis. With RTB, that same dentist can limit the ad to webpages that represent an area that's within fifteen to twenty miles of his or her office. Not only that, but, with RTB, you can also target specific pages on specific sites. For example, that same dentist might only want his ad to appear on the Invisalign page of a dental information site – and RTB can make that happen. Pretty powerful marketing stuff.

And it gets even more powerful when RTB is applied to mobile devices. It has the ability to leverage consumer data on those devices and track users just as marketers do on PCs. Location and demographic data get layered on top of real-time ad requests, so when a consumer is traveling in the vicinity of your business, you can potentially sell directly to them when it's most convenient for them to buy from you. RTB can also be used for video ads, allowing you to more fully demonstrate and sell your products and brand.

RTB is a perfect complement to retargeting because, while retargeting goes after consumers who are already aware of you and what you do, RTB is busy creating that awareness for those who may have no idea you even exist! Of course, it's very, very, *very* difficult to sell to a customer who doesn't even know you're in business, but RTB solves that problem by presenting your ads to online and mobile users who match up with the demographic group most likely to buy from you. That, in turn, gives you an increase in your Brand Lift, making your business more of a player in searches on your business category.

How Anyone Can Use Retargeting and RTB

Clearly, retargeting and RTB are insanely effective online marketing tactics – but, at the same time, they can be highly challenging and complex instruments to master for most businesses (and even some marketers who aren't up to speed with the latest online technological tools).

That's why we've built a real-time advertising platform, Traffic Oxygen (you can find out more about it at www.trafficoxygen.com) to help our clients take maximum advantage of retargeting and RTB. A company only has to provide us with their information and we can run the show from there, providing a constant and robust marketing presence that leverages the massive amount of online information that's already out there to target the most lucrative leads that match up with a specific business.

If you believe online marketing isn't all-important these days – and we'd like to have a long talk with you if that's the case – you owe it to yourself to check out the Dynamic Duo of internet advertising, retargeting and RTB. Together, they provide a one-two punch that will create brand awareness, increase website traffic, and boost conversions.

And aren't those goals every online marketing wants to achieve?

Facebook Marketing

10 Super Tactics You Need to Know to Sell to the Biggest Online Community Available

By Jeremy Howie

As If You Didn't Know Department: Facebook is a HUGE opportunity for every Marketing Avenger. With 1.13 billion daily active users on average, any advertiser can have access to what's easily the largest pool of potential buyers on the internet. But figuring out the best way to leverage Facebook has its own challenges, due to its arcane algorithms and rules.

Enter Jeremy Howie, our fearless Facebook Avenger, swooping in with just the chapter you need to save the day – not to mention your campaign!

Jeremy has made it into Facebook's "inner circle" of advertisers with whom they share exclusive information – so few people under-

stand the social media site's marketing strategies better than he does. He's directly managed over $3 million in FB ads, worked in over 50 different niches, and reached over 100 million people internationally and seen how they respond and engage – so he knows what it takes to attract leads and convert them to sales. In the next few pages, he's going to reveal his top secret tips and tricks for making the most of those billion users – so listen up. Because you're about to gain access to some real online marketing gold.

- Richard Seppala

DO YOU KNOW WHY the Facebook interface is primarily blue?

Well, one big reason is that Mark Zuckerberg, the founder of the social media site, is red-green colorblind – so he preferred a color he could actually identify.

That's a Facebook fact I can readily share, because it's fairly common knowledge. But there are a lot of other FB facts I'm legally prohibited from disclosing because of my position as part of Facebook's 2016 SMB (Small-Medium Business) Council - one of thirteen advertisers out of over three million chosen for that honor.

I gained that status with the FB folks because of the powerful results I've helped my clients achieve by marketing on Facebook. I've put six years and a lot of hours into understanding what works – and what doesn't – when implementing an FB campaign, and Facebook has only helped me increase my expertise by bringing me in as an inside advisor. As a result, I've learned a lot of amazing and confidential inside information about the site's current and future marketing strategies.

There are few, if any, venues that offer so much potential for marketing campaigns. As of the moment I'm writing this, Facebook has over 1.65 billion monthly users and is the most downloaded app on all smartphones. About seventy-two percent of adult internet users visit Facebook at least once per month and the average user spends twenty or more minutes per day on the site. It also now owns Instagram, which is over 500 million users now. Between Instagram and Facebook, the two sites control one minute out of every five that users are spending online. They own eyeballs and they own people's time – and isn't that what you want as an advertiser?

There's also the fact that you can literally reach anyone, anywhere with Facebook. You can reach them in their bed, in their kitchen, in their living room – or at their office. Everyone's carrying around Facebook in the palm of their hand on their smartphones, because the site has made it a priority to be mobile-friendly.

That's a lot of marketing superpower that everyone wants to leverage in their favor. Well, I'm going to help you do that – and, while I can't tell you everything I know about how Facebook makes things happen, I can offer you ten great "Super Tactics" on how to maximize your ROI from your next FB campaign.

Super Tactic #1: Use Video

Facebook is uniquely optimized for video. And more and more, that's how people are consuming content on the internet – there are over a billion hours of video watched and eight billion videos viewed every day by consumers. Another important fact to understand is that, according to Nielsen Research, up to 47% of the value of a video campaign is delivered in the first three seconds. In other words, you have to hook your viewer in that three seconds and you also have to do it *silently,* since they auto-play on FB without sound. As a matter of fact, your video should be telling a complete story visually without sound. That's why you see more and more videos with dialogue and narration actually subtitled, so people can watch even if they're in a situation where it's inconvenient to hear the audio. Mark Zuckerberg himself said Facebook will be "mostly video" by 2019.

Super Tactic #2: Use Mobile

As I've already mentioned, Facebook has made being mobile-friendly a priority, which has helped fuel its explosive growth. Part of that effort is making itself uniquely optimized for *mobile video.* So, if you're going to take one thing away from this chapter, it's this: **Implement mobile video on Facebook.**

In 2015, mobile-only internet users surpassed desktop-only users for the first time in history. During that year, during the traditional blockbuster shopping day after Thanksgiving, Black Friday, mobile accounted for fifty percent of all purchases, which represents a huge increase over the old days when desktop purchasing dominated. And it's a trend that's only going to grow.

For example, it's now possible for consumers traveling near a business to receive their ads on their smartphones, FB ads that even feature a "Call to Action" button that puts through a phone call directly to the local business. And it's amazingly affordable. You can get your message in front of a thousand people right now for about a $3 ad expenditure.

You can also get a lead form inserted into someone's news feed – and the user no longer has to go to the trouble of typing in their email address to give you their contact info, it's imported automatically by Facebook once the user agrees to it. We've seen our clients' lead costs cut in half because of this new system; it's so easy for the consumer to participate, they don't have to painfully type their info out for the advertiser, they can just submit it with a tap of their finger.

One final note: A great way to figure out how to target a person is to just take one look at what's on the homepage of their smartphone. See what apps they have installed and you'll get a good idea of what the person's interests are and what they enjoy.

Super Tactic #3: Use Attraction Marketing

This particular tactic goes for any form of marketing, not just Facebook campaigns and enables you to attract the person most likely to buy from you. First, define your avatar – i.e. that type of person who would be most interested in what you're selling. Give that avatar a name, an age, an interest and a location where you're most likely to find that person. Now, in your marketing, offer your avatar *value* through education, entertainment, inspiration, emotion, humor...whatever will attract their interest. Think about what they might want to see in their Facebook newsfeed. Lead with value, follow with a sale. And never, ever spam!

Super Tactic #4: Engage Through Posting

You should be posting on FB during peak time at least once a day, five days a week (if you don't know what your peak time is, you can find out if you have a Facebook page set up for your company – just check your Page Insights and see when most of your fans are online). As I mentioned already, always use videos and images (to me, straight text posts are a waste of time) – and always be thinking mobile. Also, remember you can schedule when your posts appear ahead of time. If you'd like to check out my free video about how to schedule your posts, you'll find it at this link: www.enlightenedmarketingllc.com/fbscheduling.

After you've posted, your work isn't done. You want to make sure and "like" and reply to all guests' comments on your posts. People want to be heard. If you respond, acknowledge them and thank them, they'll be much more likely to (1) come back and comment again, and (2) give their friends positive feedback about you. That being said, don't be afraid to delete negative spam or irrelevant comments – or take it offline. I have horror stories where I've seen a business and a customer go back and forth for hundreds of comments about an issue, in full view of other visitors to the page - why?

Super Tactic #5: Develop a Content Strategy

Think about your avatar again and then think about the piece of content that's going to be valuable to them. It could be a blog post, an infographic, a video, whatever – but once you have that content idea, put it on Facebook first and then integrate it into other online platforms you're active on.

For example, let's say your content piece is a video. You put it on your Facebook page, then "Boost" it out to your target audience from there. You then take that video and put it on YouTube, Instagram, wherever else you have an active presence. Then transcribe the video content and repurpose it into a blog post with the video embedded. Now you have a blog post that can get ranked on Google's search engine. You can then send that blog post with the embedded video out to your email list.

Whatever your content placement sequence ends up being, develop it into a standard operating procedure and put each content piece on an autopilot schedule. You can use virtual assistants to help you carry it out and make sure the content gets distributed and repurposed per your SOP.

Here's another tip – if you want to know what kind of content is most popular, most shared, etc., go to Buzzsumo.com to get a lot of incredibly valuable data that will help you promote your content to the max.

Super Tactic #6: Try Out Different Ad Objectives

With Facebook, you can have all kinds of different ad objectives – you might want to gather "likes" for a post, you might want to drive traffic to a link, or rack up video views, retarget, or actually convert someone to a sale. There are many, many exciting, new and innovative possibilities that the site offers which you can take advantage of. For example, you can even have Facebook become your partner in selling – you can calculate that a conversion is worth, say, $50 to you, bid that much and tell Facebook to go get you as many conversions as it can for under $50.

You have a whole lot of options – so take advantage of them by trying them out and seeing which works best for your particular marketing strategy. Follow up by testing how well your objectives were met and move on if another objective might work better for your end game.

Super Tactic #7: Split-Test Everything

I hear a lot of other marketers say, "I tried Facebook – and I fell on my face, it didn't work." Then I ask some follow-up questions: "What was your ROI? What was your brand lift? How many people did you add as a result?" The answer is too often, "I don't know, it just didn't work."

Marketing is at its core mostly a numbers game - and Facebook gives you an immense amount of reporting options to get those numbers. For example, FB can tell you what percentage of your video was viewed by how many users. You can get incredibly deep with the numbers with Facebook Reporting.

Here are a few of the most important things to split-test: Images. Videos. Creative copy. Ad Objective. Offers. You can split-test Facebook vs. Google, Pinterest, LinkedIn or any other social media platform you do paid ads on. The key is to split-test only one thing at a time.

If you're not familiar with split-testing, it's a simple concept. Let's say you run a basic ad that asks the user to check out your new product. You keep that bare-bones headline the same, but rotate five different images over the course of seven to ten days (a good testing period on Facebook). Go back and see which image had the lowest cost per click, the highest cost per click, and the most conversions for the lowest cost – then use that image. Next, you go back and test five different headlines. Over time, you come up with the most effective marriage of image and copy – and move forward with a super-powered Facebook ad that will convert like crazy!

Super Tactic #8: Use Facebook Data, Reports and Settings

As I just mentioned, Facebook has an immense amount of reporting options. As a marketer, this is a huge gift. The magic is in the numbers, so use them. And integrate Google analytics so you can confirm the data. Through this system, you can calculate things like a customer's lifetime value. Too many companies look at an individual sale as the be-all and end-all. But through Google Analytics and Facebook Reporting, you can see that a $50 sale may have resulted in acquiring a customer who will return and buy from you again – resulting in maybe a lifetime value of $20,000. It's an important number to determine and one I help our clients figure out on a regular basis.

The point is, you can glean an incredible amount of data on any buyer, Facebook has over 1500 data points on each user. They literally know everything about their activity on the site – which can seem a little scary. But for a marketer, it's information that only exists to connect your product and services with people that want to buy them. So don't be put off by the immense data pool. Instead, use it to your advantage to provide value to your avatar.

Super Tactic #9: Use Retargeting

Retargeting is the highest converting form of advertising that exists. Here's what it's all about: Say you go to Amazon and you look at a set of golf clubs. You don't buy during that visit and go on to do other things. Then, when you go on Facebook a couple of days later, you discover you're getting fed ads for golf clubs in your news feed, the same ones you were eyeing on Amazon! No, it's not a coincidence - it's *retargeting*. You've expressed interest in a product, and now you're being reminded that, hey, maybe you still want to buy this thing.

Why is retargeting so important? Well, in the past, it took four to seven impressions to close an online sale. Now, because people are more adept at ignoring banner ads and the like, that number is up to seven to fourteen impressions. Retargeting makes sure you reach that magic number and have the best shot at converting.

Retargeting is done through a process called pixeling that enables you to catch the data of a person visiting your page. If you use Google Chrome, you can get a really cool tool called Facebook Pixel Helper and you can even collect data on visitors to your competitors' pages! You'll also find out that 90 to 95% of those competitors aren't using Facebook marketing or retargeting – giving you a huge advantage over their marketing.

Super Tactic #10: Use Facebook's New Features

Facebook is always coming up with new features and tools, so always keep an eye out for their next great innovation and see how you can apply it to your marketing. One quick example: Their new private voice messaging feature. If you friend somebody on Facebook or they friend you, and they're a networker or someone in your potential target market, here's a new tool Facebook Messenger provides to really make a personal connection. You'll see a little microphone icon on Messenger now – and all you have to do is click on it in order to be able to record a voice message to that new and potentially important friend. It's much personal and more impactful than the standard typed message – and it sets you apart.

What to Expect

What's coming next in the Facebook universe? Well, here's what to expect next (assuming it hasn't already happened by the time you read this): Virtual reality will be launched and integrated into Facebook, who recently purchased Oculus, the leader in VR. I think that's going to be huge, personally. I can see people having board room meetings in, for example, a beachside environment, even though they're sitting in offices in the middle of a snow-covered winter somewhere. Now, imagine being able to market in those virtual landscapes, so that if someone turns and looks at a CGI palm tree, there's a small ad on it that they can actually click on.

There's a lot more coming from the social media "giant of giants," but, for now, let me leave you with three powerful Action Steps you can take right now to improve your FB marketing skills.

Action Step #1: Define your avatar: Determine who are you marketing to and what they want.

Action Step #2: Produce at least one short video each week that provides your avatar *massive value*. There's an easy way to get eyeballs on that video that you may have never tried before, it's called

Boost, and you can do it right from your page. Just invest $5 in a Boost and you'll see good results. The new Facebook Live feature is an excellent way to do this (https://live.fb.com/).

Action Step #3: Do a retargeting ad to people viewing your video with your product or service, so you can actively convert.

I'll admit that much of what you read in this chapter is skimming the surface. To be honest, this material needs a whole book (and then some) to be properly explained. But if you like this information and want more, Facebook puts out an amazing course available to you absolutely free called Facebook Blueprint, which you can access at www.facebook.com/blueprint.

I also have a free offer that can be of some help: A PDF download with some more great, useful information on FB marketing that's my gift to you. Access it at:

www.enlightenedmarketingllc.com/specialfbgift.

And remember, Facebook is THE social media phenomenon of our time. If you're not marketing on the site already...you should be!

My Laws of Attraction: Motivating Leads to Come to You

By Kent Littlejohn

If you're looking for a boring marketer with nothing interesting to say, RUN – do not walk! - from this chapter!!!

Sure, Kent Littlejohn used to own an insurance company, and that's not usually the most exciting profession in the world. But Kent's business caused him to have one of the most dramatic experiences I can imagine – one that threatened to tear his world apart a few years ago.

Well, his pain is now your gain; because, as you'll read in this chapter, Kent had to frantically find new leads for his business or face financial ruin. The systems he uncovered as a result literally saved his life – and they can also do wonders for your bottom line.

His first name may be the same as the last name of Superman's mild-mannered secret identity, Clark Kent – but trust me, Kent Littlejohn is the real Man of Steel when it comes to super-powered, game-changing marketing.

- Richard Seppala

LAST YEAR, A CLIENT LITERALLY said to me, "You changed my life."

Hey, you can't help but get pumped when you get feedback like that. Of course, I'm happy to hear from any satisfied client – I even have a few who've told me how I've added hundreds of thousands of dollars to their yearly revenue.

But, I have to be honest. The words "You changed my life" had a special power when I heard them.

Why? Because I had to change my *own* life before it completely crashed and burned. I had to uncover a new way, to attract quality leads, those who could afford to pay me what I needed to make, and it had to cost virtually nothing because I had no money at the time. If I couldn't make that happen, my family's future was bleak as hell.

They say great things can come out of great disasters. It's not an idea I would have subscribed to before 2012. But it's sure something I believe in now.

Let me tell you about it and share a few of the secrets I learned as a result.

That Day I Suddenly Owed 4.7 Million Dollars

In 2011, my insurance company sold over $8 million worth in insurance premiums.

Life was good. In late January of 2012, it looked like it would get even better. My wife told me a third child was on its way to join our other two. We were prosperous and happy.

Ten days later, we discovered that our lives were built around a massive fraud.

A well-known, trusted insurance executive in the industry marketed one of the most popular policies I sold. The policy was specifically for apartment building owners and had the best coverage in the business – for a very reasonable premium. A few of my buyers filed some small claims, $25,000 or so and those claims were paid promptly. There was no reason to worry.

Except this executive turned out to be the Bernie Madoff of the insurance business.

All the premium money I paid him was actually being wired to an offshore bank account in China. That meant the policies I had sold represented no insurance coverage. Zero. They were fakes. The guy paid off a few small claims so he would be trusted long enough to amass millions in premium payments.

It wasn't until February 1st, 2011 that I discovered I was on the hook for $4.7 million in debt to my clients for their fraudulent premiums.

Nobody thought I was actually guilty of anything. The fraudster was eventually caught by the FBI and sentenced to ten years in prison. But I was the guy who sold the policies to my clients. Over the next 40 days, they filed roughly 40 lawsuits against me and my company. And obviously, I lost all that income.

Suddenly, I didn't know how I would pay the rent on my office. Suddenly, I didn't know how I was going to provide for my wife and kids. Everything in my life was suddenly at stake and I fell to my knees, wondering how I would get out of this gigantic hole I had just got thrown into.

But I couldn't give up.

I knew this kind of catastrophe could literally destroy my family – which is why one of the first things I did after I had my first tough phone call with the Department of Justice and the FBI, when I first found out about the 4.7 million I was responsible for, was to hold my wife Beth tight and tell her, "No matter what happens, no matter where we end up, we're going to be all right." From that moment, we worked as a unit and never, ever had an argument about what was going on in front of the kids.

Rising from the Ashes

After about a week of walking around in a depressed daze, I said to myself, "I have to turn this around. And I have to do it now." And that ushered in a pivotal point in my life when it came to business: I decided to do it differently than I ever had before. I had to. I couldn't count on existing clients or referrals from them after what had happened, so I needed an all-new client base and I needed it fast. I needed leads, high-end leads, to *want* to do business with me – even though they had no idea who I was.

So I ran an experiment on a very established website. And, within a week, I had locked down four new clients. Four BIG new clients. That's when I knew I was on the right track – because I now knew how to rebuild my business and rebuild it fast. Unbelievably, at the end of 2012, I ended up almost breaking even. Amazing. And then the next year, we started making money. Big money.

My new lead generation systems were working so well that, at the end of 2013, I turned to Beth and told her I wanted to sell the insurance business. After all we had been through, it obviously had lost a little luster for me. Two years later, on the anniversary of the worst day of my life, I sold my insurance business for seven figures. A comeback I never expected – but one I never stopped working towards.

To put the cherry on the cake, I now had a new business that was much more satisfying and rewarding to me personally. It began when a buddy of mine reached out to me, after he saw my amazing results. He wanted to know how I built my business back up from rock-bottom so quickly. He was in a completely different marketing niche than me, so I had to think, "Will this actually work for anybody else?" But, hey, there was nothing to lose for either of us. So...we tried it out.

Within a few weeks, he was having massive success on his side too.

It was super-inspiring to see that happen. That's when I knew that I would have a lot more fun, and get a lot more personal satisfaction, out of offering the systems I had come up with to others like me. Suddenly, I was able to help thousands of business owners, salespeople, and entrepreneurs all across the globe.

And suddenly...I was thankful about getting left holding that 4.7 million-dollar bag. After all, my insurer finally did take care of most of that bill – and I now had a new and much more fulfilling business to run.

Putting Together My Marketing Miracle

So how did I come up with my lead-generating systems?

The obvious answer is they came out of desperation. But, as a result of that desperation, I found myself unable to settle for anything that didn't deliver miraculous results. Because of my horrible situation, I suddenly assumed a mindset that demanded instant success. My new marketing plan, whatever it ended up being, had to meet three huge – and I mean, huge – requirements:.

Requirement #1: Speed

Since I didn't have money coming in, I needed new clients *yesterday.* And most entrepreneurs would tell you that getting new clients so quickly was impossible. After all, it takes years to build a business, right?

That was a conventional way of thinking that I couldn't afford. I had to think getting new clients immediately was doable. And that meant I had to grow beyond the traditional small business marketing approach based on *hunting.* With hunting, the marketer goes out in the world, tries to get the names of some interested leads, and then goes after them one at a time, selling to each over a period of time until they were finally ready to buy. But I didn't have time for all that. I had to do things differently.

Requirement #2: High-End Leads Ready to Buy

If you're a business owner, I'm sure you know how exhausting it is to work a lead for a number of weeks (or even months!) until you wear them down and they agree to do business with you. And that's just the moment where you might find out they never could afford you in the first place! It's time and energy you can't get back – and it results in a high level of frustration to boot.

But how do you make sure a lead can realistically work with you? Ask for their tax returns and bank balance information? Of course not, but I had to find a way to identify viable leads. I couldn't afford to waste my time on people that were never going to buy from me.

Requirement #3: Finding a Simple, Powerful & FREE Networking System

Finally, I needed to identify a powerful and already-existing platform where I could easily identify and network with the kind of high-end leads. I didn't have time to find the right "mix" of Google PPC ads, Facebook and Twitter posts, etc. that would create the exact right online strategy – I wanted to focus on one platform, the right platform, where I could make my mark quickly.

The platform I decided on was a platform that many marketers overlook – LinkedIn.com. Most view LinkedIn as just a series of glorified business cards and not much else. Well, what I discovered was *it was perfect for me to market to high-end contacts.*

There's a basic different between LinkedIn and other social media sites. If someone's on LinkedIn, they're serious about doing business. When somebody logs on Facebook, however, they're posting pictures of their family, their cat and maybe a vacation they just returned from. LinkedIn users? They're there to *do business.*

And many of them are capable of doing a lot of it.

The average person on LinkedIn is earning six figures, $110,931. In other words, it's where people with money are hanging out. You've got 3 million people on LinkedIn that are CEOs of companies - and that doesn't even include CFOs, CMOs, COOs and all those other O's. Those O's might resemble zeroes, but they added up to a lot of capital.

That's why I decided that LinkedIn was my dream marketing platform. And I'm happy to report that I was absolutely right. With LinkedIn, I was able to act quickly to identify high-end leads and reach them with very little effort. Along the way, I discovered 99% of the LinkedIn users didn't really understand how to use the site the most effectively – the way I was using it – which gave me a clear advantage with what I was doing.

My "Laws of Attraction"

My LinkedIn networking system has three "legs" to it – authority positioning, lead targeting and client attraction. In the remainder of this chapter, I'd like to talk about the third, client attraction.

I'm going to share some of the powerful strategies I used (and continue to use) to attract high-end clients. As I mentioned, the whole point was for me *not* have to go out there and hunt for them, but to find ways to have them approach *me*. Here are a few of my "Laws of Attraction" that helped me – and continue to help my clients - realize awesome results.

Law #1: Keep It Real

If you want to attract people, you first have to make yourself attractive. Makes sense, right? Well, that process begins by being transparent about who you are and how you do business.

What do I mean by being transparent? Simple - just let people know who you are. If you like to travel, post information about your last few trips. If your family is as important to you as mine is to me, work that into your profile and your writing. All of these everyday things link you to people on a very human level. People buy people, of course, so it's about getting them to like you, not your company - and then building an authentic relationship based on who you are as a person.

And that extends to the way you sell. In the past, you'd find a lot of photos of online marketers posing by a Lamborghini in front of a giant mansion promising you unlimited riches if you follow their advice – and, in most cases, they come off as the posers they usually are. That kind of flaunting causes people to distrust you before you've even made contact with them. Worse yet, this kind of overblown marketing usually doesn't attract quality leads; instead, you get people who want to get rich quick - but are definitely not rich now!

So present yourself as credible and trustworthy, but be yourself. That kind of authenticity lowers resistance on the other end and it also makes you feel more at ease in your business dealings. You don't have to try as hard - and when you don't try so hard, it makes you even more attractive to prospects.

Law #2: Mirror Your Ideal Client

Let's say I want to hire a coach, and that coach's price is $5000 a month. Let's say I want to lowball him – so I offer the guy half of that, $2500.

Well, wait a minute...do I want *my* clients to try and do that to me?

No, of course, I don't. So why am I doing that to this coach? And if that's how I put myself out to the world, then aren't those the kind of people I'm going to attract in return? Don't I get known for being the guy who does deals – and doesn't that mean everyone will assume they can do that kind of half-price deal with me? I don't need that kind of reputation – I'll just spend most of my time trying to justify my fees!

That's why, out in the world, I try to represent the perfect client that I would want to work with - because it will naturally attract that kind of person back into my life. It can be exhausting to work with people you don't really match up with – you don't get them and they don't get you. It's nobody's fault, but it's what happens when your approach is wrong. Your reputation always precedes you, so use a high quality approach in the business world. You'll be seen as a high-quality business person and attract that level of client in return.

Law #3: Never Stop Looking for Opportunities to Connect

Finally, never overlook an opportunity to monetize even the most innocent networking.

For example, recently it was my "work anniversary" (something I'm willing to bet few people really celebrate). When a LinkedIn member has one of these anniversaries, the site makes sure everybody hears about it. In my case, LinkedIn messaged all my contacts that Kent Littlejohn was celebrating his 2nd year at Core Digital Marketing.

And it asked people to congratulate me.

In response to that type of LinkedIn automated message, many users set up their own automated response to be sent out on the same day. That meant I got a ton of pre-fab messages that all said something like, "Congrats on the anniversary! Hope you're doing well."

This complete lack of actual human input didn't put me off. Instead, I quickly wondered how I could use these automated messages from my contacts to my advantage. So I wrote a short note back to all of them - a note that thanked them for the congratulations and added, "If you'd ever like to connect with qualified leads here on LinkedIn, I hear we're pretty great with that!" And then I added a smiley face as an end button.

Well, we generated multiple deals from that.

It may be too much to say the LinkedIn saved my life. Maybe I should just limit it to saying the site saved my bacon. Whatever the case, it helped me pull off an incredible turnaround that still takes people's breath away.

I know what the stress of waiting for your next client can feel like. And it's awesome to help the coaches, consultants, entrepreneurs and small business owners I work with eliminate that stress. If you're interested in hearing more about what LinkedIn did for me – and what it can do for you – I invite you to contact me.

I'd love to help you change your life too.

Becoming a YouTuber

Creating Celebrity and Marketing to Millions

With Mackenzie Senters

I have to admit something. I'm old. I'm not talking senior citizen old, but, let's face it, it's been over two decades since I've been out of high school and there's a whole new generation coming up behind me, ready to rock the worlds of marketing and entrepreneurship as they've never been rocked before. And I thought that it was important for that generation should be represented in this book.

That's why I'm happy to present a conversation I had with Mackenzie Senters, our youngest Marketing Avenger, who is currently a "YouTuber" – a personality who records their own videos on their own YouTube channel. If you're thinking, "What's the big deal about that?" let me tell you about a young guy named PewDiePie. Not familiar with him? Well, he's the number one YouTuber – and last year he cleared over $12 million from the social media site! NOW maybe I've got your attention!

Mackenzie Senters has only just begun to build her video empire in the making, but she's got a lot to share about this exciting new kind of online marketing. So, without further ado, enjoy my talk with this fierce and fashionable online marketer.

- Richard Seppala

Richard: So tell me a little about yourself, Mackenzie.

Mackenzie: I'm 19 and I'm a student at the University of Kentucky.

Richard: 19. You are definitely our youngest Marketing Avenger! What inspired you to start your own YouTube channel?

Mackenzie: Well, I was already thinking about it when I went to a marketing seminar a few months ago with my dad. I went to learn about marketing and also to talk to business people. There were a lot of entrepreneurs there with their own individual companies, so I thought they would really inspire me and teach me a lot about how to go about what I was planning. And from that seminar, I saw how I could not only create my own YouTube channel and blog page, but also run it like a business.

Richard: What was the big takeaway you got at the seminar?

Mackenzie: The big thing I learned is to that you have to put yourself out there. Don't be afraid, you might as well give it a try, because if you fail, it's not a big deal. It doesn't hurt you in the long run and you learn a lot from it.

Richard: And if you succeed, you can do really well in this arena. I was recently reading that YouTubers are actually becoming more influential than normal celebrities. 70% of teenagers say they relate more to YouTubers than movie, TV or pop stars and 4 in 1 millennials say YouTubers understand them better than their *friends*. So there's a lot of potential in what you're doing. Tell me a little about your YouTube channel and what you do on it.

Mackenzie: It's called StandTallWithKenzie and I just started it a few months ago. I post videos on the channel about beauty, health, fitness and fashion. I love all those things, I've learned a lot about them and I just want to share what I like with people out there.

Richard: Were there any other YouTubers doing the same thing that you liked? Ones that inspired you?

Mackenzie: Casey Holmes is definitely one. Then there's Jaclyn Hill and another one with a channel called "GlamLifeGuru."

Richard: Have you always been interested in fashion?

Mackenzie: Definitely. When I was little, I loved to wear big bows. I even sponge curled my own hair when I was only four. My mom always dressed me in the girliest things and I really enjoyed it. But then I went to private school, where we had to wear uniforms – so I really wasn't able to show off my individual personality with my clothes. That made me lose some confidence, along with the fact that I quickly shot up to 5'10" – I ended up being taller than all of the boys for a while!

But in 8th grade, I went to public school again and I was able to wear what I wanted. But, like I said, I had lost my self-confidence, so I mostly just followed what everybody else was doing with their looks. It wasn't until near the end of high school that I actually went back and created my own style again.

Confidence is so important. As a matter of fact, my blog is going to be more about confidence than what I'm currently doing on the YouTube channel, which is more style-oriented. I feel like it's easier to write about that than to do a video about it. But that is a big goal of mine, to help people be confident. That's why I named my YouTube channel, StandTallWithKenzie – since I am confident and tall, I stand tall now. And I want my audience to stand tall with me.

Richard: So what's your process? How often do you record your videos?

Mackenzie: At the beginning of each month, I write down a list of ideas that I want to do videos about. But that's just for back-up. I shoot my videos every Tuesday and, if I can't think of what to do that day, that's when I go back to my list and pick a couple subjects from there. I try to post twice a week, usually on Wednesdays and Fridays.

Richard: Do you script out what you're going to do?

Mackenzie: No, I just do it! I just wing it.

Richard: Now, when you actually post the video, what tags or keywords do you attach to your videos?

Mackenzie: My most important tags are when I use a specific product in the video. If, say, I'm using a make-up product for example, I tag the video with the product name. I created an Amazon Affiliates account, so if somebody is interested in the product I'm using and goes and buys it through my link, I get a small percentage of that sale.

Richard: So that's one way to monetize it. You also get paid by YouTube when you get a certain number of views on your videos, right?

Mackenzie: Yes, but I've only been doing this for a few months, so I'm not at that point quite yet.

Richard: I'm sure you will be. What other social media do you use to promote the videos?

Mackenzie: I'm on Facebook, Twitter, and Instagram and I also use Snapchat a little. When I post a video, I put it on my Facebook "StandTallWithKenzie" page and let my followers there know a new video is up. I'll also post a picture on Instagram and promote the video there. Since there's such a big gap between videos from Saturday to Tuesday, I'll post a reminder or two during those down days.

Richard: A lot of people are self-conscious when they make a video with themselves on camera. If you don't have experience on camera, it can be a pretty intimidating process. Had you done videos like this before you started the YouTube channel?

Mackenzie: No, not at all.

Richard: So, when you made your first one, were you nervous?

Mackenzie: Yes, I was nervous and I felt really awkward while doing it. At first, I thought I wouldn't actually talk on-camera. I would put on the make-up or whatever, and then, later, I would add a voiceover of me describing what I was doing and giving tips to whoever was watching. Then, when I did it the first time, I kept wanting to talk while I was putting on the make-up, so I could describe what I was actually doing. I ended up redoing it a few times, until I finally realized it was a lot easier and a lot more natural if I talked while I was doing it. And that's the way I do them all now.

Richard: So I guess your parents must be supportive – your dad was the one who took you to the marketing seminar in the first place, right?

Mackenzie: Yes, my dad has been pushing me to do this for years, since I was in high school. But I never listened back then, because that's what you do when you're a teenager – you ignore what your parents tell you, right?

Richard: In one ear and out the other. How about your mom?

Mackenzie: Oh, she thinks it's awesome too. She's really excited about the blog I'm starting too, because, in addition to talking about confidence, I'm going to do a lot more fashion-related stuff there and she follows the same fashion bloggers that I do.

Richard: How have your friends reacted? They can be a tough audience, right?

Mackenzie: The great thing is that all of my close friends I've had since high school are really supportive. And there's this one girl I know from college and one day, she randomly texted me about something. And when she was ending the text conversation, she mentioned, "I think your YouTube channel is really awesome and I'm so glad you're doing it." That was great to hear.

Then I have another friend from college who is happy I started the YouTube channel, because she wants to do some videos with me! She's really into social media and wants to team up with me on some stuff.

Richard: Are you going to do any with her?

Mackenzie: Yeah, I think so. There are a bunch of different types of videos that you can do with a friend. You can do a blindfolded makeup challenge, where you blindfold your friend and she tries to apply the makeup on you – that can get messy. Or you can do a best friend tag, where you ask the other person questions about yourself that she should know the answer to – and then you see if she gets them right. So I've been thinking about it, yeah.

Richard: Well, it sounds like you're off to an amazing start with your YouTube channel, Mackenzie. I wish you all the success in the world. Is the blog site up yet?

Mackenzie: I'm just about done setting it up and it should be up in a few weeks.

Richard: Well, by the time this book is published, it should be live. So, for everyone reading this, you can check out Mackenzie's blogsite at standtallwithkenzie.com and her videos at

www.youtube.com/channel/UC24PHkK-u9m5D70JUiTYn6A

Keys to the Crowd

Unlocking the Power of Crowdfunding

By Brandon T. Adams

This is a big year for crowdfunding – the year that funding from such sites as Indiegogo and Kickstarter is projected to surpass money raised from traditional Venture Capital for the first time in history! It's just another way that the internet has turned business upside down in a flash - which is why most entrepreneurs out there still aren't savvy about making this powerful new online money-raising tool work for them.

Enter our own "Captain Crowdfunding," Brandon T. Adams.

Brandon, a super-successful entrepreneur and inventor, has mastered the art of crowdfunding to help himself as well as others finance all kinds of new projects – and, lucky you, he's here to share his secrets with everyone reading this book. If you're looking for capital, then here's a capital idea – read on and find out how crowdfunding can finance your business dream!

- Richard Seppala

IS THERE ANYTHING MORE frustrating than creating a successful product – and not having the financing to properly bring it to market? I know what that pain feels like – because I experienced it myself. But, then again, that difficult situation opened up an amazing new avenue of fundraising for me – crowdfunding. Learning how to make crowdfunding work for me has become my biggest business "super power."

Here's how I acquired this extraordinary skill.

I grew up in a small town in northeast Iowa, where my father sold packaged ice for a living. It wasn't until the summer of 2011 that I came up with an idea while delivering ice for my dad's company.

I called the idea "The Arctic Stick" – a product you could insert into bottled beverages that cools and flavors them (you can check it out on Amazon, where it's sold). I felt like this invention could really take off, but, of course, you need money to develop something like this. So, when I graduated from college, I raised about ten grand from family and friends to get it started. I paid it back and worked two jobs to keep the idea going – but then I hit a real brick wall; I needed about $25,000 to pay for the tooling and machinery to mass-produce the product.

And that's when I realized, for the first time, that crowdfunding might work for me.

I went on Kickstarter.com and did my very first campaign. And I did literally *everything wrong*. And even though I had no idea what I was doing, I raised a little over $26,000 in 33 days – just enough to get Arctic Stick to market.

But the crowdfunding opportunity stuck with me. I investigated some more and found out that 65 to 70% of campaigns failed to raise the money that was needed. I also discovered there was no expert out there helping people with this relatively new and insanely great online tool.

I decided I wanted to be that expert.

In 2015, I spent the whole year traveling and talking to people who really killed it on Kickstarter, and raised millions. I learned so much, I ended up writing a book about it (*Keys to The Crowd: Unlock-*

ing the Power of Crowdfunding, also available on Amazon) and starting a new company, also called Keys to the Crowd, to help others crowdfund. In November of that year, we set out to raise money for an Entrepreneurial event called Young Entrepreneur Convention, for which we raised about $16,000 – with crowdfunding, of course. That allowed us to attract tens of thousands more in sponsorship money to put on the event, which led to it becoming one of the largest entrepreneurial events in the country, with close to 500 attendees. Inc.com even named it one of the top 5 most innovative new conferences to attend in 2016.

Then came a real success story. Our company helped put together a Kickstarter campaign for John Lee Dumas, whose "Entrepreneur on Fire" podcast regularly gets over a million listeners. We raised $27,000 in two and a half hours. Then, we hit $58 grand in 12 hours. $100,000 in 33 hours. And finally, by the end of the 33 days of the campaign, we reached $453,000.

And that was my real lesson in how powerful crowdfunding could be – when you did it *right*.

My Formula for Crowdfunding Success

So *how* do you do it right? How can you make sure you not only reach your financial goal – but easily surpass it?

In this chapter, I want to reveal my Formula for Crowdfunding Success, which is based on this simple acronym:

- Forethought
- Utilize Marketing Plan
- Narrative
- Deliver Value

Let's go through each of the above "ingredients," so you can understand what the formula is all about.

Forethought

Simply put, forethought is everything you do to prepare before your campaign even begins – and I suggest you start getting ready anywhere from 45 to 60 days prior to launch.

What should you be doing? Creating a landing page to promote your campaign all the way up to day 1 and also creating the campaign page itself. And that involves choosing the right visuals, writing compelling copy to tell your story and explain why you need the money, and producing a video to get people excited about your project or your cause. These are all the critical components for your landing page, which should detail when the campaign begins and also prominently feature a "Subscribe" button which will allow visitors to get information about your crowdfunding effort.

Just as importantly, you want something to motivate them to *hit* that Subscribe button. Advertise exclusive offers, such as half off a product (we'll talk more about other incentives later). The purpose of this promotion is to build up your email list, which is all-important; that's why we spend thousands of dollars on Facebook targeted ads to direct people to our landing pages. This whole pre-campaign effort is to get people to feel committed to your campaign, so you can have an amazing launch on Day 1. A successful crowdfunding campaign will raise 30 to 40 percent of the total funding goal in the first 48 hours of a campaign – and the only way that happens is if you get people committed and excited before you launch, and give them a REASON to contribute as soon as the campaign begins.

That's why you want to build up your email list – because, the day before launch, you want to let them know that if they give on Day 1, they can get to a certain pledge level at a discounted rate (and enjoy bigger benefits as a result). You can only do that with a substantial audience in place *before launch ever happens.*

The truth is, if you don't get a lot of traction right at the start, your campaign can easily fade out and die a quick death. Kickstarter and Indiegogo, like most websites, use an algorithm that takes into account the number of pledges, the amount of money pledged, and the number of visitors to your page to determine your ranking in the websites' search engines. If you rank high, those search engines will deliver more people to your campaign page – and it could mean tens of thousands of new eyeballs looking at your pitch. I've talked to people who have raised $150,000 in 24 hours because they were ranked high in the algorithm on day 1 and were sent out to the email list for Indiegogo (this list is HUGE) which led to many backers in a short period of time.

Wouldn't you like to enjoy similar results?

Utilize Marketing Plan

Next, you need to have a marketing plan in place to get the word out about your campaign through other outlets. One of the best ways to do that is through what I call an "Ambassador Program," where you get influencers on board to help spread the news about your pitch.

How does an Ambassador Program work? Well, let's say you want to raise money for a fitness product. What you should do is try to contact celebrities in the fitness industry and reach out to them. Ask them to be ambassadors by helping to support your campaign with their followers. For example, they can send an email out to their list, they can share links on their Facebook, Twitter and other social media accounts and, if they have a podcast, they can have you on as a guest.

Of course, you need to find a way to reward them for being your ambassadors – and you can do that by promoting them and their offers. You can feature links to their websites and put their picture on your campaign page, or give them some kind of unique access to your crowd or free products. You can even encourage them to be affiliates and set them up with special links – links that they feature on their websites and social media which will deliver them 10 or 20 percent (the number is up to you) of whatever they raise for you through their followers. I've found the Ambassador Program is a huge component to crowdfunding success.

Another great marketing method is packaging news stories for traditional media. This is something I've been successful with in terms of getting myself featured on radio and TV shows and in newspapers. You have to give them a story that seems timely, maybe just by resonating with the time of year or a location where your campaign is going to happen. Do as much of their work as possible by writing up a professional article or press release and getting it to them. Reach out to as many on- and offline venues as possible. Blog. Get on podcasts. Do everything you can to get attention close to your launch date, if not on the actual date itself.

Finally, think about creating some punchy 10 to 15 second videos that you use in paid advertisements on YouTube, Instagram and so forth. Make sure your video has an embedded link that will take them to your campaign page. Short videos work the best, because people just don't have the attention span to watch something long and complicated; but a longer form video should still be definitely part of your campaign and part of your landing page.

Narrative

The most important aspect of that long form video should be a strong narrative. Storytelling is a huge part of selling anything; when you can tell a good story, you can get people excited about your product or service. Crowdfunding is no different, you want to tell a great story and draw in subscribers – and the best way to do that is through a high-quality video.

This long form video should be under three minutes with decent production values, especially good, clear audio – and you should also do something *within the first five seconds* to grab the audience's attention, so they'll want to keep watching. Depending on what your campaign's subject matter is, you can do something funny or outrageous, you can ask a provocative or compelling question or jog the viewer's mind in some other way; it's up to you. Then, within the first 30 seconds, you want to clearly state what you're doing, what you're asking the viewer to do and what they're going to get in return if they pledge. For the rest of the video, focus on three to four attractive features of the product, service or project, and then, at the end, give them a small Call to Action, where you tell them specifically what you want them to do – pledge, be a part of something new and exciting, etc.

Overall, your mission with narrative is to make your campaign seem like an opportunity people can't resist, an opportunity with a BIG component to it. Throughout your crowdfunding web page, continue to tell the same story through copy, visuals, infographics, testimonials, and whatever other resources you have. Be consistent and stay close to whatever storyline you've decided on.

Deliver Value

The final aspect of my FUND formula is "Deliver Value," where you answer the question, "What's in it for me?" Any potential pledger has to feel there's a reward for helping you out with their hard-earned money. Truthfully, this is where many crowdfunding newbies make a crucial mistake – they assume people are going to give them money without any strong incentive. No, it doesn't work like that – *people always want something in return.*

So if you're crowdfunding for a product, give pledgers a heavy discount, 30 to 40%, when it's finally available for sale. Make it a very exclusive or limited time offer. If you're crowdfunding for something other than a product or service, tailor the incentive to whatever it is you're raising money for. For instance, we have a campaign going to produce a reality show – so we're offering people who pledge ten grand or more their own segment in one of the episodes. Basically, you have to give them something that's unique for the experience. If you're a celebrity (or a celeb is involved somehow), maybe the top pledgers get to spend a day with the celeb. Whatever you come up with, make sure it's creative, attention-getting and, most of all, delivers *value*.

The Benefits of Crowdfunding

There are several HUGE benefits to crowdfunding and here are just a few.

You raise the money you need. Pretty obvious, but it bears repeating: You get the money you need for the project you want, if you follow the FUND formula.

You don't give up equity. You gain investors without having to relinquish any control whatsoever to your company. You're raising money without strings attached. And that's the best way to get it.

You don't go into debt. Many entrepreneurs and business owners end up feeling like they're swimming with one hand tied behind their back, simply because they are forced to take on crippling debt to get the funds they need to do business. Not a problem with crowdfunding.

You get your business important publicity. If you do the crowdfunding process correctly, you end up attracting media attention and tapping into a whole new audience for your venture, which leads to our next benefit...

You build up your company's valuation. By gaining that much new attention, you attract other valuable business opportunities for your company. After a campaign, I frequently have *more* investors approaching me wanting to put money into the company. I've also attracted wholesalers, licensing deals, and other important offers that made my company more valuable than it was before.

It's easy to do more crowdfunding in the future. If you want to introduce a new product or service, or expand on what you're already doing – well, guess what? You still have that email list of subscribers from the last go-round, which gives you a built-in base for a new campaign.

You get valuable feedback. Finally, since you're only at the beginning stage of creating an actual product or service, you can get incredibly good guidance from the people who pledge money. After all, they're the folks who are interested in the kind of thing you're raising money for – and they can tell you what they'd like to see happen with it. You can even get the sense of if a product will fail – and save yourself the time and money of actually moving forward with an idea that nobody wants.

As I said at the beginning of this chapter, crowdfunding is my biggest business super power – and the great news is, it can be yours too. You can easily learn "The Keys to the Crowd" and tap into the vast online audience out there to make your business dreams come true. Just follow my FUND formula – and you too will be enjoying all the massive benefits that crowdfunding can bring to YOUR company!

The Mobile Revolution

Boost Your Appeal
with an App

By Aaron Ayotte

You'll find that with many superheroes, their power is in their hands – literally! Want proof? Just check out where Spider-Man's web, Iron Man's repulsor rays and the beam from Green Lantern's magical ring all spring from. With that in mind, it just follows that we'd have a Marketing Avenger who would have a similar handheld weapon, right? Right.

That Marketing Avenger's name is Aaron Ayotte, and his handheld weapon is the mobile phone. Statistics show that more and more consumers are accessing the internet mainly through their mobile devices – so it just makes sense that marketers should focus their online efforts on smartphones, tablets and the like.

As Aaron is about to explain, mobile apps make it amazingly easy to increase customer engagement, repeat business, loyalty and impulse buys. Not only that, but your logo becomes a permanent part of their smartphone wallpaper! If you've been avoiding implementing an app for your business, Aaron's going to show you why NOW is the time to go mobile – and how easy it is to make happen!

- Richard Seppala

WHETHER YOU'RE PACKING an iPhone, an Android smartphone or still rocking a Blackberry, odds are that not only is your mobile device an integral part of your business life – but it's also essential to your personal day-to-day existence.

That's pretty much what research tells us anyway. The latest study, done by British psychologists, estimates that young adults are on their phones, doing one thing or another, for an average of five hours a day. That's a third of their waking hours!

Okay, so maybe you're not on yours 24/7, but I'm am betting that you still rely on your smartphone to get a whole lot done, including scheduling, social media, email, texts, news, get the latest sports scores, play your favorite games, get the weather forecast and...oh yeah, maybe even actually making a call!

With all that in mind, if you're an entrepreneur or marketer, it just makes sense you'd want to make yourself an integral part of any kind of technology that's critically important to your consumers – especially when you consider these marketing statistics:

- According to Juniper Research, many people spend more when they use coupons they receive on mobile devices.
- Americans who use shopping apps on their smartphones are using them for an average of 2 hours, 5 minutes per month, according to Nielsen.
- Americans spent $838 million online via mobile devices in one single day – Cyber Monday in 2015 – and that figure was up more than 50% from the previous year, according to comScore.
- A Loyalty360 report shows that mobile is extra effective in reaching millennials.
- Mobile can also help business owners trying to boost foot traffic to their stores. Juniper research reported that 56%

of smartphone users would like to receive location-based offers on their phones.

All of the above numbers make it clear that smartphones are probably the smartest place for you to not only bond with your best customers, but also expand your overall marketing power. I agree. And that's why I'm going to explain how I found my foothold in this fantastic new field – and how apps can add so much to your business.

Putting Apps on the Map

If you ask most people how they got into the business they're in, they'll say it was kind of an accident. That's just how it was for me.

When the housing bubble began to burst in 2007, foreclosures starting growing like wildfire – and a lot of homeowners needed help. I made it my business to help them avoid losing their entire investment in their houses. We got in the trenches for them and dealt with the banks holding the mortgages and helped out with short sale negotiations when necessary. Many, many people needed our help at the time and we became very successful in our efforts.

During those years, I met somebody who built a very powerful software platform that enabled our company to go paperless – and manage all the document and contract flow on computers and through the internet. Because of that connection, I ended up on this guy's email marketing list – and one day, I received a message from him talking about the growing mobile marketing opportunities that were out there. I was invited to a webinar he was holding to find out more.

I decided to check it out. Why? Well, I knew the foreclosure wave was going to eventually fade and I would need to shift gears. Since that business would soon be in the past – what was going to be in my future? Well, after I watched the webinar, I knew I had to give mobile marketing apps a try. At the time, I was living in a small community in Colorado, with only 5000 people. It was beautiful there – but the town itself was tiny. I thought to myself, "If I could sell apps in this little town – where the average age of residents is 57 – this kind of business will work anywhere."

That next day, I went downtown, walked in to a local restaurant and introduced myself to the owner. And I talked about making an app for his place. After we met for an hour, he committed to buying an app on the spot, which was a good news-bad news situation for me. The good news? If I could sell this idea on my first try, it definitely had promise. Bad news? I had yet to take the time to figure out how much I could charge for an app!

I finally settled on what I thought was a reasonable price, the restaurant owner agreed and I decided to try my luck selling one to another local business. I told that owner about my first sale. He responded, "Rob got one?" I said, "Yeah," and that was enough to motivate him to buy one too. This time around, I raised my price by 30%. He didn't bat an eye. Two weeks later, I sold my third app to a business in town – and hiked my price by another 30%.

This was obviously a popular idea.

The problem was, apps would reach a saturation point very quickly in a town this size; that would mean people would start getting annoyed by every business asking them to download their app and stop using them. My solution? Build a single app where you could access all the businesses in town and charge those businesses to be a part of it for a low recurring fee. I let the first few businesses I sold apps to get in on it for free. I ended up with 19 businesses in all signing up for it. The app would allow them to provide digital coupons, run rewards programs and a lot of other marketing goodies.

Now, even though there were only 5000 people in the town, the place attracted millions of tourists in the summer. So, to launch the app, I had 10,000 business cards printed up with info on how to download the app; then, in the middle of July, my wife, kids and I went all over town handing them out to visitors and sticking them on car windshields. Result? 2500 people ended up downloading the app – and using it to find the best places to eat, stay a night or two, get a drink, whatever they wanted to do in our small town.

One of the great advantages of the app for local businesses came with the off season. During those quiet months, the lodges and hotels used push notifications (which I'll talk about soon) to reach all those tourists from the previous summer – and remind them to book for a trip next summer before. Before the app existed, those tourists would have come and gone without any of the local businesses having a way to market to them afterwards. Now, with the app, they could reach all those warm leads with just a click of a button. They were psyched about this incredible new way to keep track of customers and continue to communicate with them.

All in all, my first big app venture was a huge success; around 6500 customers still regularly use the town's app. And even though I've moved on, I've allowed all those businesses who helped me get my start to keep marketing through the app for free.

Now, a few years later, the power of mobile apps has only increased by leaps and bounds since then. I was reminded of that power today, as I was putting gas in my truck at the local convenience store; there, on top of the pump, I spotted a brand new sign advertising the store's Rewards Plus app where regular customers like me can take advantage of their loyalty program. And I thought, is there any company that doesn't have an app these days?

Well...maybe yours doesn't. And if that's the case, read on for why it should!

Why Mobile is a Huge App-ertunity

First of all, marketing is about engagement – reaching people where they're spending the most time and are the most likely to interact with you. As I've already mentioned, people are spending a huge amount of their time on their phones – so what better place to reach them? And what better place to connect with them?

Usually, marketing is very two-dimensional – whether it's an ad on a bus stop or a commercial on television, it's usually a very one-way method of communicating. With an app, however, it's an ongoing conversation. Someone coming into a business discovers it has an app, downloads it in the store, and immediately starts taking advantage of any coupons or rewards programs they offer through the app, without wasting any time. They don't even have to carry around any rewards cards – they can access a rewards program through their phones, which they're going to carry around with them anyway. And that's just the beginning of the benefits for both business and consumer, since the communication can continue wherever the user goes – because wherever the user does go, they're more than likely taking their phone with them!

For your part, your business suddenly has a very easy and efficient way to carry through on your marketing efforts. You don't have to print coupons or those rewards cards I just mentioned – and your employees don't have to worry about distributing those kinds of materials or dealing with loyalty programs. It all happens virtually, no muss and no fuss.

And updating your marketing efforts is a breeze. It's easy to change up your digital offers, add features to your Rewards Program, change your prices, revise your products and services, whatever you need to do. You don't have to spend hundreds of dollars printing out a coupon – only to find out later the coupon wasn't really pulling in any customers. Instead, you just change up the offer on the app and send out a push notification to alert your customers.

By the way, push notifications are another HUGE advantage to mobile app marketing; they really increase engagement and keep every app user informed on just what you're up to, even if your app isn't open on their phone. That's because a push notification is like a text message; whether it's an iPhone or an Android device, a user gets notified of your message on the phone's home screen – and the message can contain a link that, with a quick touch of a finger will take the user to the web page of your choice or open your app automatically to provide more info. That allows you to send out "app-only" special deals that users will appreciate and take advantage of.

Why is communicating with your customers through push notifications so important? There's no question that email marketing is very powerful - it always has been, and it's still a very inexpensive and efficient way to market to your customers. One of the challenges, though, is that email has a pretty low read rate; everyone's inbox, these days, is inundated with marketing emails and yours can easily get lost in the pile-up. Depending on what you're selling, emails only have a read rate of between 4 and 15%.

On the other hand, everyone has their smartphones close at hand – either in their pockets or actually in their hands. Which is why push notifications have a 97% read rate. They're short and show up on the phone screen – so it's hard to avoid reading them!

Apps can also tie into social media, yet another red-hot virtual place to engage your clients and customers. The app can link right to a company's Facebook page, Twitter, Pinterest, you name it. It's all connectable to whatever suits your type of business best.

Another great thing about mobile apps is they're a great way to pump up a slow business day. We've built apps for hair and nail salons and other walk-in businesses which they can use to offer last-minute deals that can stimulate foot traffic. For example, say it's slow on a Tuesday and the manager turns to an employee and says, "God, it's dead in here. Let's send out a push note." Suddenly, everyone with their app gets notified that the next ten haircuts are ten dollars off. How else can you do that kind of instantaneous marketing with such a guaranteed read-rate? The answer is there is no better way! You could send an email, but many people might not check their inbox until later that night – and that's too late to solve your slow afternoon. Facebook, same thing – as a matter of fact, your post could get pushed down users' newsfeed to the point where they might never see it! But a push notification will get read almost immediately – giving you the best chance at generation extra business

Finally, another great use for marketing apps is having customers leave reviews through them. For instance, you might tell a satisfied buyer, "Hey, you know, we have a free smartphone app. Since you had such a great experience, we'd love it if you installed it on your phone and left us a review right on our app." You or an employee can then walk the customer through the process and explain how to share their review on social media or wherever. It ends up being another powerful piece of engagement.

Optimizing Your App

I've talked about the obvious ways you can use a marketing app. But there are a lot of other creative ways you can use yours to deliver an awesome experience to your customers – as well as a powerful profit to yourself.

For example, one of our clients is a restaurant in New Orleans whose app we're retooling, because they're upgrading their delivery service with an aim to provide a fast, delicious lunch to any business for only 7 bucks per person. If a group of employees want to order lunch in an easy way, without a lot of hassle, they just go through the app. Each person picks an entrée and two sides on the app, and it's all processed through the phone with a PayPal payment without any actual paperwork involved. The old days of having to find a menu, finding the restaurant's phone number, getting a list of everyone's orders and slowly and painfully reading the whole thing over the phone are over. All those archaic steps are just gone. Now you just punch in the info and – boom!

As I write this chapter, I also have a huge project going with a different industry that maybe you wouldn't expect to have an app - the heating and cooling sector. Big air conditioning companies like Carrier are working with us to provide apps for their dealers to help them sell more of their products. When these dealers repair someone's air conditioning, they can advise them about the app and their rewards program. It's an easy way to increase engagement; the dealer can make sure the customer comes back to them for their next service call, and the customer has an easy way to remember the company he used (and to get rewarded for using them again!).

It's all up to you on how you can best optimize a mobile app for your specific business goals. Just know that, whatever those goals are, a mobile app provides the best and easiest way to engage your customers, reach out to them with special offers and make sure they keep coming back to you for more!

Millions from Mailboxes

The Secrets Behind Successful
Direct Mail Marketing

By Craig Simpson

Can a superhero save the marketing day – by mail? Believe it or not, the answer is a resounding "YES!"

For those of you who think the U.S. Mail system has lost all of its power in this internet-centered time, meet Craig Simpson, the Iron Man of the Mailbox! In this chapter, he'll explain why direct mail is far from dead – and may just rescue your next marketing campaign!

Richard Seppala

I'VE HAD **18** YEARS OF EXPERIENCE working in the direct mail industry – and I estimate that over that time, I've sent out over 200 million pieces of mail. You would think that in itself would be enough to keep the post office afloat.

What I've learned through those years is just how much direct mail marketing can do for a business – when it's implemented correctly. It can literally generate millions for a company – I've seen it happen with my clients (and I'll reveal how one did it a little later in this chapter).

Currently, through my company Simpson Direct, I send out almost 300 mail campaigns a year for a variety of business niches – everything from huge companies like Beachbody to information marketers, clothing wholesales and even small dental and chiropractic practices.

I work with my clients to come up with the right story to deliver their marketing message. I then oversee the copy and design of the mailing and then select the right mailing lists. I also coordinate the printing and mailing and also track the response from each campaign.

Because I'm so closely involved in the entire process, I've gained the experience to understand what works in direct mail and what doesn't. And because I do have that informed perspective, I believe I'm able to give my clients their best shot at success with their direct mail campaigns.

In this chapter, I'll share some of my expertise – and a lot of my secrets – on how to make the most profitable direct mail campaigns happen for you.

Why Direct Mail Over-Delivers

Of course, now that we're in the 21st century, where almost all communication is virtual or electronic, some make the mistake of questioning the relevance of direct mail. "Snail mail" in general does not get a lot of great press – mostly because people hear about the Post Office's struggles on a regular basis. And yet, marketing through the mail is a *growing* business, not one that's going away anytime soon.

Here are a few of the undeniable advantages of direct mail marketing:

Less Competition for Your Leads' Attention

Obviously, people don't mail as many personal notes or letters anymore. Who needs to pay for a stamp when they can use Facebook, email or phone texts to send a message? That may be bad news for the postal service, but it's good news for direct mail marketers. With fewer letters in the mailbox, the recipient pays *more* attention to what does get sent to them. Your mailed message has a much greater chance of being read now than it did a few years ago.

A One-On-One Audience

When a person checks their mailbox, pulls out your mailer and sits down to take a look at it, you've got him or her all to yourself – with no other distractions. With TV, you've got another commercial before and/or after yours, if the viewer even sticks around to see your ad. Online, of course, you've got a million marketing emails invading in-boxes alongside yours – if you made it through the "spam" filter.

Statistically, of course, email open rates keep going down and online sales keep getting tougher to make. That's where the real competition is - and why it's so hard to make your message stand out. You don't have those problems with direct mail.

The Ability to Segment and Target

When you're marketing through other media, often you're just using a shotgun approach – blasting everyone at once to see if you actually are lucky enough to connect with a potential customer.

With direct mail, however, you're able to send out your mailing to the exact niche market you want to hit; today's data-mining services are able to provide an incredible amount of information that enable you to zero in on your most likely customers. For example, if you're selling golf equipment, you can do a mailing to a list of high-income golfers who would be more disposed to buy from you.

Higher Quality Buyers

This is a huge reason to go with direct mail marketing – because it means you'll realize more money from your marketing over a longer period of time. I've found that customers that were converted through direct mail marketing spend more money and remain more loyal over the years.

To confirm this, I did a test with a large publisher in the real estate market a few years ago. We marketed to 50,000 leads through direct mail, 50,000 different leads through TV advertising and 50,000 more through online marketing. The product being sold was a real estate course, sold at the exact same price through all three methods, over 18 months.

When we looked at the three different groups of prospects, we discovered that the TV buyers had a lifetime value that was twice as high as the online buyers – and that the direct mail buyers had a lifetime value *three times* as high as the online buyers (and close to twice as high as the TV group). Those are amazing numbers and testify to the ability of direct mail marketing to connect with the exact kinds of customers most marketers are desperate to reach.

How to Make the Right Impact with Direct Mail

A little later, I'm going to share a huge secret I've learned to achieving success with direct mail. But first, I want to review a few of the basics that are important for anyone considering a direct mail campaign to know.

First of all, as note, you have to do the right demographic research to make sure you use the right mailing list for your campaign. Targeting the right recipients for your message makes a huge difference to your response rate.

Secondly, when it comes to your message, you want to make sure you're selling your product or service in the right way. Many marketers make the mistake of focusing on *features* instead of *benefits*. With sales copy, that's a big no-no.

For example, let's take Crest Whitening Toothpaste; people don't really care that it contains stannous fluoride, glycerin, hydrated silica and sodium hexamethaphosphate (not to mention xanthan gum). No, they care about how well it will brighten their teeth – which is how Crest advertises it.

So don't concern yourself so much with what you think are the cool features of your product or service – focus instead on what those features are going to do for your potential customers. Be benefit-oriented, rather than descriptive, and you'll motivate more purchases.

Finally, especially if this happens to be your first direct mail campaign, you want to make sure that the *format* you choose for your mailing is the right one for the leads you're sending it to. You can choose from literally dozens and dozens of different types of mailing formats - including such options as an eight-page sales letter, an oversized postcard, or a booklet or digest-style informational piece. You have to decide which format best suits the message you're trying to deliver.

For instance, if your ultimate aim is to just drive someone to your website, you don't need 12 pages of copy to achieve that goal. However, if you want to sell a health supplement through the mail and the goal is to get the lead to spend ninety dollars on something that's designed to help relieve joint pain, then a postcard is not going to provide nearly enough information to make that kind of sale happen.

Your best bet is to see what other successful marketers are using in their direct mail campaigns to sell similar offers. If they're getting the response they're looking for from their campaigns, consider a similar format for your product or service.

The Real Secret of Million-Dollar Direct Mail Success

As I said, I have years of experience with direct mail campaigns, so I've obviously been able to learn many important lessons about how to use direct mail to its fullest potential. And to me, the biggest secret of all is really in how you define the objectives you set for a direct mail campaign – mostly in terms of whether your objectives are long-term or short-term.

Most of the time, a marketer will make the mistake of judging the success or failure of a direct mailing by how much revenue they made off an initial sale – instead of evaluating the lifetime value of a new loyal customer they may have found as a result of their campaign.

For example, let's say you have a dry cleaning business and you mail out some postcards in your local area to introduce yourself to potential new customers. And let's say, as a result of that postcard, ten new customers come in and spend about $35 apiece on a first order. Now, you might look at that and say, "Whoa, I spent a ton of money to make $350?"

But that's the exact *wrong* way to look at it. Because if at least half of those ten people keep coming in month after month for the next few years, all of a sudden that $350 multiplies by many times over – especially if the new customers like your service and recommend you to their friends and neighbors.

When you understand marketing, you understand the enormous value of gaining new long-term customers. Unfortunately, I've dealt with many, many businesses who don't realize this – and who fail to grasp the fact that, with every marketing campaign, you have to calculate your ultimate ROI based on the lifetime value of a new customer, not on an individual sale.

That's why many of my clients expect a short-term loss on their direct mail campaigns – especially if they're information marketers. For example, they may be selling a niche financial newsletter or a real estate course Maybe they're selling whatever the product is for $127 – but it costs them $185 to acquire the customer through direct mail. The average person would say, "Well, that's silly, they're losing money, not making money – why would they do that?"

But the average person isn't looking at it from my client's perspective – a perspective in which they know the lifetime value of those customers is going to be around $500 per person. When you do the math that way, they're really spending $185 to make $500 – which, of course, makes a great deal of sense.

In other words, direct mail is a way to get new customers in the door – and, hopefully, keep them there. And that brings us to the second and most important part of this direct mail secret, which is **doing follow-up mailings.**

Again, this is a case of long-term thinking versus short-term thinking. When you're only thinking of making one sale from a customer, you may think you don't need to do direct mail with that person again – you can just email offers to them at low-to-no cost.

What my clients see the most success from, however, is *not* changing up their mode of marketing. Direct mail worked with this person – and it will work again. So why not do a *follow-up* direct mail sequence to continue to sell more?

This was the exact formula for success for one of my largest financial clients that I work with, The Ken Roberts Company. We did an initial direct mail campaign for them in which we sold over 700,000 courses through the mail at $195 apiece. The course was on "How to Trade Commodities" - and, as soon, as someone bought it, we would, over the next 17 weeks, then follow up with 11 more mailings to the same person. Each mailing would contain a different offer.

Yes, that's a lot of mailings, a lot of work, and a lot of expense – but those mailings helped the company grow to the point where it was making over one hundred million dollars a year, with 95% of that business being driven through direct mail.

That's all due to performing follow-up mailing just the way I described. The Ken Roberts Company would acquire a customer through the initial mailing we'd do for them, and then we would follow-up with those people with more offers.

If someone buys from you the first time, odds are it's because you've directly hit on an important interest of that person's. It could be a professional interest or it could be a personal one, like a hobby or side venture. Whatever it is, it's something they're willing to take out their credit card for and, again, they'll probably continue to do just that for products that are along similar lines - as The Ken Roberts Company proved over and over again.

If I were to sum up this crucial secret of direct mail marketing, it would be like this: It's crucial to recognize that *if they respond to you once, they will respond to you again.* And if it's not you continuing to pursue them and selling them something else that appeals to their primary interests, it will be your competition.

You may not know this particular historical fact, but the first person to ever use direct mail marketing was Benjamin Franklin back in 1774, when he sold technical and scientific books through a mail-order catalog. Starting the direct mail industry may not have been as important as his discovery of electricity, but it's definitely powered many a business success over the last two hundred-plus years.

If you're interested in finding out more about what the right direct mail campaign can do for your product or service, feel free to email me at craig@simpson-direct.com to get a copy of my 16-page report, "7 Proven Ways to Profit from Direct Mail." Just mention that you read my chapter in Richard Seppala's book, and I'll send the report to you at absolutely no cost.

The Secret to Massive ROI and Growth for Any Business

By Shaun Buck

Are you ready to make a buck? Then talk to Shaun Buck. Actually, you don't even have to talk to him, just go ahead and read this chapter!

In his guise as the Newsletter Pro, this Marketing Avenger spurs business growth and boosts ROI with the simplest of marketing tools—the newsletter. It's so simple, its critical importance to lead nurturing and customer retention is often overlooked. But the information Shaun presents in this chapter will refocus your attention on this moneymaker PDQ!

- Richard Seppala

WE HAVE ALL BEEN TOLD THAT 15 PERCENT year over year growth is good; 25 percent is killing it. And you know what? They're right — that is good growth. But what if you want more? What if you don't want it to take five years to go from a million-dollar business to a 2 million-dollar business? How are some companies achieving 100 percent, or even 1,000 percent growth rates? What you'll discover in this chapter are the secrets that allow companies to grow at extraordinary rates.

I first discovered the secrets to massive growth when I was in my early 20s. At the time, I really loved business and learning about business models. The business model I was most drawn to back then was franchising. On the surface, I still feel franchising is super attractive. Think about it! Here you have someone who has started a business, had success (hopefully), figured out systems for running day-to-day operations, planned the marketing strategy, built a customer base, and, heck, they even figured out which vendors to use. Now, after doing all this work, they've gone out and sold franchises to dozens if not hundreds of people. Those people then found success and hopefully sent back additional ideas and even improvements to the franchise system. With all this work done, ongoing support, and a model that is a proven winner, it's easy to see why I thought franchising was the way to go.

Because I strongly felt that franchising was the surest path to success, I did a ton of research on the subject. I would order the legal documents (at the time, they were called UFOCs, but now they are referred to as FDDs) from dozens of franchises that I had some interest in and would read these documents for fun. Although the thought of reading legal documents may not sound like fun, there are some great lessons you can learn from this review. For example you get a bit of insight into the business model and how the franchise operates. You'll also get to see the sales process of each franchisor. How these guys sell is very instructive, as many of them suck (a great lesson in what not to do). But a few of them actually have a process that includes a "shock and awe" package, follow-up, scripted phone calls, etc. In short, a process that *works*.

When I was looking for my second franchise (I was around 22 years old at the time), I ran across a company called Dry-Cleaning-To-Your-Door. It seemed like an interesting business model, so like any franchise I thought was interesting, I ordered the UFOC documents. Now, the lady who had founded the company and who was selling the franchises didn't have an amazing sales process. She didn't have the best shock and awe package—heck, she was the lone sales person and had little, if any, training—but what she did have was a long-term follow-up system, and it became one of the keys to her success.

The system started with a shock and awe package ... but without much shocking and very little aweing. Basically what she sent was a glorified sales letter, a newsletter, and the ugly legal documents that everyone was required to send. This package was not unlike many other franchisor packages, but where she differed in her process was the long-term follow-up. You see, she called and sent me additional direct mail and emails on a very regular basis.

One of the main pieces she sent out was a monthly print newsletter. Each month, when this eight-page newsletter came in, my wife and I would devour it. To be honest, I devoured it, then I made my wife read it so we could talk about all the things in it that I was excited about.

Quite honestly, and a bit surprisingly, this newsletter did everything right. The newsletter had success stories of new and existing franchises, as well as a franchisee top 10 list to showcase the system's best franchises. The newsletter had information on best practices and even highlighted the upcoming franchise convention. Each month, these newsletters would come; then the company founder/saleswoman would follow up with me via a phone call. And each month, I would get more and more excited about the opportunity.

Now, one of the reasons it took so many months of follow-up for me to decide whether or not to make the purchase was that I had another two-location franchise I needed to sell to have the money required for purchasing this franchise. But after reading the founder's newsletters for a number of months, and with the upcoming franchise convention rapidly approaching, I decided to call Uncle Discover and Aunt Visa, take a loan, and make the plunge to buy a Dry-Cleaning-To-Your-Door franchise.

It took nearly eight months from the time of my request of information for me to make my decision to purchase. Although that may seem like a long period of time, it ended up being about six months sooner than I had originally expected. One of the key reasons I decided to buy early was the constant and consistent communication that caused me to get more and more excited about the opportunity.

Out of the many dozens of UFOCs I requested, Dry-Cleaning-To-Your-Door was the only franchise that followed up with me on a regular basis, continuing to tell me their story and about all the cool things going on in the franchise system.

One of the reasons 99 percent of businesses don't grow very fast is that they give up on their leads far too early. Each one of the franchisors that I spoke to on the phone knew I was in the research phase of my buying process. I explained to all of them that I was looking for a new business because I was in the process of selling my old one, and I needed to finalize the sale before I'd have the money to purchase their business. Even though I was very upfront about my timeframe and intentions, most of them never contacted me more than once or twice after I requested information from them. This is exactly what most businesses do (possibly even your business), which is why most fail to achieve the success they desire.

The Truth About Making Sales

One of the things I love about big companies is that they have the money — and the man power — to do research smaller companies can only dream of. Moen Faucets is one of these big guys, and they've created a system that gives great insight into the buyer time-line.

So here's their buyer experience and how they structured their research.

Surprisingly, not everyone just goes to Home Depot when they need a new faucet. Many people actually request information about the different faucets they're interested in before they make a purchase. When someone sends an inquiry to Moen Faucets, the company, of course, sends out the requested information and then conducts what's called a buyer survey. The survey is pretty simple; every 90 days, someone makes a phone call and asks the potential buyer, "Did you buy a faucet?" If the answer is yes, the prospect is marked as a purchaser and is then asked, "Did you buy a Moen faucet?" If the answer to the first question is no, they haven't made a purchase yet, Moen notes that no purchase has been made, then they call you back in another 90 days.

What Moen found is amazing. When someone requests information about your product or service, 15 percent of them are ready to buy within the first 90 days of requesting information. Now, most businesses don't follow-up for 30 days, let alone 90 days, but let's put that aside for a moment. The rest of the study found that 51 percent of all people who request information about a product or service will make a purchase in that category within 18 months of requesting the information. This means that two-thirds of all your leads that come in today won't be worth anything for up to 18 months from now. And, to add insult to injury, most of those leads will have long forgotten about you and your business over that 18-month period. So a lack of follow-up is the same as sending the money you spent on lead generation down the drain.

Here's what it comes down to: It is your job to remind your customers and prospects of who you are, what you do, and that you're still in business. It is not their job to remember.

Insight into sales person follow-up shows that the average sale closes on the following attempts:

- 2 percent of sales close on the first call
- 3 percent of sales close on the second call
- 4 percent of sales close on the third call
- 10 percent of sales close on the fourth call
- 81 percent of sales close on (or after) the fifth call

If you want to increase your ROI, you have to increase the number of attempts you make to close the sale. And if you want to drastically increase your ROI and speed of growth, you must follow up with different media over a minimum of an 18-month period.

3 Secrets for Growing a Business 2,975 Percent in 3 Years

The company I own and operate today is not a franchise, but I have to thank, in part, the franchise I spoke about earlier for sending me down this path. My current company is The Newsletter Pro (a far cry from the dry cleaning business), and we write, design, produce, and mail custom print newsletters. Over the last three years, despite claims of print and direct mail being dead, my company has grown 2,975 percent, which landed us at spot No. 120 on Inc. Magazine's 500 list of fastest growing privately held companies. Since making the list, I've been asked dozens of times about how we grew that fast and what our secrets are. I pondered this for some time, and now I'm ready to share our secrets for crazy-fast growth.

Secret No. 1 — We Don't Give Up On Leads.

When you get on my list, we chase you. Not in a creepy stalker way, but in a relationship-building, trust-fall way.

For example, each month you'll get a print newsletter and a few emails from us. Like I said, nothing crazy, but unless you remove yourself from the list or otherwise indicate you're not interested or a good fit, you'll be on our list until you buy. This approach to the sales process — a consistent flow of communication — means we sell to a larger percentage of our prospects than most businesses can hope for.

Here is a little insider look for you based on the first quarter of 2016:

- 35 percent of our new sales came from leads who were on our list for between 0–30 days.
- 29 percent of our new sales came from leads who were on our list for between 31–90 days
- 7 percent of our new sales came from leads who were on our list for between 91–365 days
- 29 percent of our new sales came from leads who were on our list for 366-plus days

Study that for a second, and you'll discover that over a third of our new sales for the quarter came from people who had been on our list for over 91 days, with the bulk of those sales coming from prospects we'd kept in contact with for over a YEAR. As we discussed earlier, most businesses fail to follow up after even 30 days. If I had taken this approach, nearly two-thirds (or 65 percent) of my total new sales for the quarter would have NEVER happened. Our monthly print newsletter and follow-up email campaigns are in place so I can stay top of mind with my prospects, which brings long-term success.

Let me ask you what would your business look like — how would your personal financial situation be different — if you were closing 65 percent more sales from your current leads?

Secret No. 2 — Retention is King.

Most small businesses don't give a single second of thought, or dollar of budget, to customer retention, which is a massive reason most companies don't see accelerated growth. The single most difficult and expensive part of any business is getting new customers. To then allow them to walk out the back door as fast or faster than you can move them through the front door is a major factor in why most small businesses don't grow — or at least don't grow very quickly. At The Newsletter Pro, we haven't had to replace hundreds of customers each year caused by massive churn because we keep a handle on retention.

If we use a basic example and basic math, understanding retention is easy. If you currently lose 100 customers per year and add 120 customers per year with your marketing efforts, your net number of new customers per year is 20 (120 new customers minus 100 lost customers). If you allocate a budget to focus on customer retention, with a goal of cutting the number of lost customers in half to only 50 lost per year, but keeping the number of new customers you get each year the same at 120 newbies, you would now grow by 70 new customers (120 new customers minus 50 lost customers). This is 350 percent faster than without the added focus on customer retention.

I could go into the math and science that shows that the longer a customer is with you, the more they spend each year, making a third-year customer many times more valuable than a first-year customer. But for time's sake, take my word on this: Focusing on retention also has a positive impact to both topline revenue and bottom-line profits. What is your strategy for customer retention? Every business has churn, but it is your job to manage that churn.

How do you fix customer attrition? A study done by The Rockefeller Foundation found that 67 percent of all customers leave a business because they feel the business (which means both the owners and employees) are indifferent to them. Remove that perception of indifference by building a relationship with your customer through something as simple as a print newsletter. This, by itself, will decrease churn, and every customer who doesn't quit and take their money somewhere else is another customer who helps you speed up growth. If you want to maximize ROI and accelerate growth, you must focus some efforts and budget on managing retention and decreasing churn.

Secret No. 3 — Maximize referrals.

Every business owner I know says they want more referrals, and although I'm sure they mean it, few — if any — act appropriately on that sentiment. I've found most people invest money and time in the things they really care about, and most businesses invest little of either in referrals. The people who are willing to pay hundreds or thousands of dollars to get new customers, but who are only willing to offer a $50 gift card for a successful referral from an existing customer always baffle me.

When you set up your business so that each new customer brings a friend with them, you have one of the major keys for massive growth. You also have a huge competitive advantage that will allow you to outspend your competition in terms of customer acquisition. That will drive them crazy because they'll never understand how you can spend what you spend to get a customer. But to get to this point, you can't be cheap. You have to invest in referrals, which includes offering a worthwhile gift to the person who is referring for you.

Don't underinvest in referrals. Don't use a "Field of Dreams" strategy where you think that if you build it, they will come. You should have a plan that includes a) existing customers, and b) the often overlooked (and possibly even better source) referral partner, who is someone who can refer their customers, clients, or leads to you on a larger scale and more regular basis than the average consumer can. I could, and have through other venues, talked about referrals and creating referral partners at length, but that is outside the scope of this chapter. For more information on referrals, go to Amazon and grab a copy of my book, titled *The No B.S. Guide to Maximum Referrals and Customer Retention.*

Maximizing ROI and creating massive growth is all about long-term nurture of the lead, minimizing customer churn, and increasing customer referrals. The best vehicle to help you achieve those goals is a monthly print newsletter. Done right, it can be the primary source for customer retention and, in turn, spell crazy growth for your business.

Referrals to the Rescue!

By Jody Layne

Having trouble generating leads? Would you like to promote your business in the most powerful way possible? Then call in the magical might of Jody Layne, whose Marketing Avengers name is "Referral Girl!" As the founder and CEO of Expect Referrals, she's built a robust, affordable and easy-to-customize referral program system that enables every business owner and entrepreneur to achieve big results with a very small effort.

Find out for yourself how Referral Girl can create awesome results for your company faster than a speeding bullet!

- Richard Seppala

IT CAN BE HARD TO KNOW what's going to be the next big marketing thing. During my eight years as president and co-founder of a major direct marketing agency, I saw a few waves come and go. Some were ultimately disposable fads, but others were groundbreaking and amazing.

I was looking to ride one of those big waves, if I could spot the right one before it crested. And finally, I saw THE huge coming marketing opportunity that I had been waiting for. Its attraction? Well, it wasn't just based on pie-in-the-sky wishful thinking. Instead, it was grounded by a perennial marketing principle that had been time-tested and completely proven – but, at the same time, there was real potential to take it to unheard levels with the explosive growth of online activity.

That opportunity ended up motivating me to leave my own agency and start anew to build a business based on *social referral marketing*. That business, Expect Referrals, has been my focus since then and I haven't looked back.

In my ROI Marketing Avenger guise as "Referral Girl," I feel confident that I'm packing some of the most powerful automatic marketing systems available today through our website at ExpectReferrals.com. If you're unfamiliar with why social referral marketing works so incredibly well – and how it can help build and expand your business to incredible heights – well, just read on and I'll tell you!

The Power of WOM

I mentioned that social referral marketing was based on a proven marketing principle. As a matter of fact, it's routinely acknowledged as one of the most effective marketing methods of all time – and it's called "WOM." No, that's not a sound effect you might see on an old Batman show when the caped crusader socks the Riddler in the mouth – it actually stands for "Word of Mouth." Study after study identifies WOM as one of the most incredible marketing tools that's at a business owner's disposal – and yet, most don't know how to fully utilize its power.

Word of Mouth, of course, is simply what happens when your product or service is recommended to someone by a friend, neighbor or family member; in other words, a person who doesn't have a stake in your business and just feels motivated to spread the good word about what you do and how you do it. That kind of recommendation is taken more seriously than an advertisement or solicitation you pay for, because, obviously, you're just trying to get more customers – so it's in your self-interest to tell people how great you are. Clearly, the average consumer is going to be skeptical of what you're telling them because of that fact. WOM, by contrast, is seemingly motivated only by someone being impressed by what you're offering.

Here are a few eye-opening statistics about WOM:

- 84% of consumers say they trust recommendations from family and friends about products – the highest-ranked source for trustworthiness, according to the Nielson research company.
- 74% of consumers identify WOM as a key influencer in their purchasing decision, according to Ogilvy/Google research.
- 68% trust online opinions from other consumers – making those online opinions the third most trusted source of product information, according to Neilson.

Pretty good, huh?

Let's face it – all of us are bombarded by marketing messages day and night. And we do all we can to avoid them. We DVR shows to zoom past the commercials, we buy satellite radio packages and streaming services so we can listen to our favorite music without interruption, just to give two big examples. Frankly, constant blasts of marketing can get tiring to consumers – even when those consumers are marketers like us!

That creates a big problem for businesses. When people out there are doing everything they can, even paying good money, just so they can avoid marketing messages, what's a small business to do – especially when it can't even afford high-level advertising? How does it differentiate itself from its competition as well as from all the other "noise" out there?

That's where WOM comes to the rescue. When we hear a friend or a family member tell us that they had a great experience at a car wash, a dry cleaners or any kind of business you can think of, we tend to listen. Why wouldn't we? These are the kinds of people we love and trust – they wouldn't try to mislead us, what would be the point?

And frankly, that's why WOM is so powerful. It's not bought-and-paid-for advertising. It's spontaneous positive comments from someone we know. And ultimately, it's a lot more effective than the most expensive television commercial money can buy.

The Referral Factor

As I said, WOM is powerful – but, as you might imagine, WOM is also hard to motivate on your own. You can ask satisfied customers to talk you up to their friends all you want, but odds are they're going to forget pretty quickly about your request. We all have busy lives and helping another business isn't usually top-of-mind, even if that business happens to be great.

But it can be top-of-mind – if it's easy to do AND there's something in it for those satisfied customers.

That's why creating a referral system with incentives in place can immediately jumpstart your positive WOM and, as a result, your sales. A couple more statistics, from the research arm of *Software Advice*:

- More than 50% of respondents are more likely to give a referral if offered a direct incentive, social recognition or access to an exclusive loyalty program.
- 39% of respondents say monetary or material incentives such as discounts, free swag or gift cards greatly increase their chances of referring a brand.

In other words, you can increase your positive WOM dramatically by having the right referral system in place – and that, in turn, will give a huge boost to your chances of obtaining new customers. It also helps increase your current customers' loyalty level. After all, why would they go somewhere else if they can benefit from staying with you and continuing to get incentives to refer you?

And by the way, there are a whole host of incentives you can offer current customers that won't break your bank account. We have tons we can recommend, including a simple discount or gift card when they refer a certain number of people, or even just setting up a discount for them at a related business who also wants to generate more leads.

That's the bare bones of why referral programs work. When you motivate a high level of WOM, it brings in a high level of new "warm" leads. But the cherry on top of this cake and what really excited me about the future of referral marketing a few years ago was the dramatic rise of social media.

Communication has never been easier in our new digital world. You can, of course, access just about *anything* through your smartphone – or *anyone* for that matter. Through Facebook, Twitter, Pinterest and all the rest, people now have their own virtual communities they can instantly and effectively reach. That's good for them – and great for you if you can get them to tap into their own personal communities and sell your business for you.

But...how do you make that happen?

The thing is, most businesses don't really know how to make social media work for them effectively. They'll post ads or images designed to promote themselves, but most social media users aren't going to pay much attention to these kinds of posts that resemble small billboards more than anything else.

So what WILL get you the right kind of attention on social media?

Referral Girl has got the answer!

Social Referrals = New Leads, New Business

At Expect Referrals, we've tapped into the amazing power of *social referrals*.

I use the term "social referrals" as simple shorthand to describe referral marketing that takes advantage of the viral WOM that occurs every day through social media sites. When you successfully motivate your customers to spread the word about your business, product or event to their friends and family through online and digital means, you can enjoy a lot of benefits that other businesses don't.

And what really makes a social referral work in that way is using some kind of *digital coupon*.

It used to be consumers had to wade through the Sunday newspaper and physically cut out coupons they wanted to use. Then they had to save them, maybe in an envelope in a drawer somewhere, and remember to actually take them along with you when you shopped. You also had to make sure you used the coupons before they expired. It was a messy, time-consuming chore that many couldn't be bothered with.

Digital coupons have changed that game completely.

By being instantly available on mobile phones and instantly redeemable, they're incredibly easy to access and use. And that's why, over the past few years, the usage of digital coupons has exploded, with double-digit growth in consumer usage occurring annually.

Once again, I'm going to throw a statistic at you to prove my point. According to *Mobile Commerce Daily*, 96% of all mobile users will search for a digital coupon in 2015. Why wouldn't they? When you can save money just by doing a quick search on your smartphone, there's no point in not doing it. So what explains those 4% that don't? I can only assume they're still using flip phones from the 90's!

It comes down to this: Everyday Americans are still finding it hard to get by – and they welcome the kinds of deals that can pop up in their social media feeds. More and more, quite frankly, they *expect* them – and go in search of deals through Groupon and other coupon sites. With social referrals, however, the coupon gets delivered right to consumers – they don't have to put any effort into finding them, the deals find them instead!

That's why, when you use a digital discount or freebee coupon in your referral program – and allow your customers to share those coupons easily on social media - it can be an incredible lead generator. For example, our Expect Referrals system allows a customer to use four different ways to share a coupon - through email, Facebook, Twitter and through a link to a personalized URL.

As I've noted, social referrals aren't just about referral marketing, they are also amazing lead generators too! That's incredibly valuable in this day and age, where it's getting more and more difficult to get your hands on great leads. For example, trying to buy viable and useful business lists is beyond expensive these days.

In contrast, social referrals are an incredibly *inexpensive* way to attract new customers who are interested in what you're offering. When you offer discounts and deals that match your potential customers' wants and needs, it's irresistible for them. As a matter of fact, as I said, they're actively seeking them out. And there you are, making it easy for them to get them!

And it IS easy for you to do just that when you use a system like our Expect Referrals platform. Once you customize it to your specifications (with our help of course), customers can continually share your incentives and refer you on their social media accounts, which can potentially expose your business to an infinite number of new leads.

Plus, since you are tapping into the power of WOM, these leads will see you a trustworthy and desirable business to buy from. We even make it possible for your customers to add their own personal message to coupons they share, so it's still a very personal delivery system. And best of all, you control the message that's being put out about your business all across the internet – so you're seen in the best possible light.

Promoting Your Referral Campaign

Of course, none of this marketing magic happens unless you take the time to promote your referral program to your customers, so they use it. Even if someone is buying for the first time from you, when you provide them with the right incentive for participating in your referral program, they not only will return and buy from you again, they'll let a whole new set of potential leads know about how awesome you are!

Unfortunately, most business owners don't have the time or know-how to do that kind of promotion consistently and correctly. They send out an email or two – which almost always end up either in the spam box or instantly deleted by the recipient along with the other 200 marketing emails in their inbox.

And that's where Referral Girl comes in handy again!

"Referral Girl" is actually a new branch of our Expect Referrals team that specifically focuses on finding easy and affordable ways to keep your referral program top-of-mind with customers without being pushy or annoying about it (we're very conscious about not letting you get lost in the marketing "noise"). We consult with you to figure out what will work specifically for you and the way you do business.

Here are just a few of the ongoing ways we help you spread the word about your referral programs:

- QR code on your business card
- Poster in your store
- Sign by the register
- Link on the Checkout page of your ecommerce site
- Print on your invoices
- Include in your email signature
- Create a social sharing page on your website
- Hand out a card with every purchase
- Print on back of your appointment cards
- Place a card in your restaurant's bill presenter
- Print the site link on pens and hand them out

And there's a lot more ideas where those came from!

The bottom line is referral marketing *works*. It's very inexpensive to put into operation and it ends up being a fantastic lead generator. If you want more general information about referral marketing, we've got tons of information on our website at ExpectReferrals.com.

And if you're looking for an easy affordable one-stop solution to creating your own social referral program and spreading the word about it, we invite you to contact us. The power of referrals is what transformed my career. I think it can also transform your revenues and send them flying...up, up and away!

Never Quit! The ONE
Way to Success

By Brad McLeod

In a lot of ways, Brad McLeod IS a real-life superhero. You're about to find out just how bad ass this guy is, not just because of his time as a Navy Seal member – but also because of what he went through to become a part of that elite team (even more elite than the Marvel Avengers, in my humble opinion!).

Brad now coaches entrepreneurs not only physically, but also mentally – you can check out his inspiring and awesome blog at www.neverquitblog.com. In this chapter, he's going to share his motivating message, a message that motivated me to get him to write this chapter for my book!

- Richard Seppala

I WAS GOING NOWHERE.

When I graduated from high school, I didn't really feel I had much going for me. I had been a C- student, which only qualified me for the local community college. I had no discipline and no athletic background at all – as a matter of fact, I had asthma as a kid and was in an oxygen tent when I was two and three years old.

So what was I good at? Skateboarding. Sure, we would skateboard across town to get to the local Half Pipe, but it wasn't like I was running track or pumping iron. And that was about it for doing anything physical.

That's what made what happened next so crazy and random. I saw a Navy Seals poster, got intrigued and read a book about them. Suddenly, it was like a switch was flicked inside my brain. I knew beyond a doubt that the Seal team was my destiny – and I made a 100% commitment to become one of them.

Which made it all the more painful when everybody I knew laughed when I told them.

The Quest

This chapter is going to be a little different from the others you're going to read in this book. I'm not going to give you details on a new marketing system or tell you how to multiply your revenues. That's all great information to have, so kudos to the other Marketing Avengers who have that kind of brilliance to share.

But me, I want to talk about *attitude* - the kind of attitude every entrepreneur needs to succeed. As most of you reading this already know, to make good with a new venture needs more than know-how and luck. More than anything, it takes persistence and guts. And it takes an unshakable belief that you can achieve your ambitions.

When I decided I wanted to be a part of the Navy Seals, I took on that type of unshakable belief – and here's how it played out.

As I said, when I shared my new dream with my buds, they thought I was being ridiculous. I was like some farm boy who went to see a *Star Wars* movie and suddenly thought he could be Luke Skywalker. The thing was, not only did I not have any military experience, neither did anybody in my immediate family, just an aunt and uncle. I had never even *met* a Navy Seal, but now, out of nowhere, I was going to be one?

Yeah, I told everyone, yeah, I was.

So I went for it. I started training – but in all the wrong ways, because I didn't know any better. I got a book - Arnold Schwarzenegger's *Education of a Bodybuilder* - which is terrific if you want to excel at lifting weights. But being a Navy Seal was all about being fast and agile – so I should have been running, doing pull-ups, that kind of stuff. Instead, there I was, working out in a bodybuilding gym with oiled-up guys in bikini trunks doing all the weight machines. What I *did* take away from the experience, however, was learning discipline and accountability for the first time in my life.

I guess that was enough to make it work for me at first. I signed up for the regular Navy and I passed the test for the Navy Seals the first time around. Only one other guy passed with me. So I was feeling pretty good about myself.

But then I had to survive Hell Week.

130 guys and me went through a solid week of the most grueling physical and mental punishment possible. I think I got maybe one whole hour of sleep during the entire five-day stretch. We were put through all sorts of drills involving swimming, running, carrying boats around on your head and getting shoved into the cold surf at night, all while they kept hammering you with the ultimate question - "Who's ready to quit?"

Well, a lot of people answered that question in the affirmative – there was a really high attrition rate. But somehow, I had the will-power to make it through all that. I was one of the lucky ones.

But not for long. Because, soon after that, I ended up getting booted from the program and probably the lamest reason you can imagine: I didn't pass the math test! My weak scholastic background had finally done me in.

The Second Chance

After that embarrassing wash-out, I was back in the regular Navy to serve out my hitch. So there I was for the next year at sea, swabbing the deck like any good sailor. It was pretty grim – but I was still determined. I kept doing my workouts designed to keep me in peak condition for the Seals program, but it was difficult to find space to do them and difficult to keep in shape eating traditional Navy grub.

And once again, I was getting laughed at.

The other guys on the ship made me the butt of their jokes. Why the hell would the Navy Seals give me another shot, when there were hundreds of other guys lined up to try and get a spot? They wanted the best and my shipmates didn't see me as being anywhere near that mark, especially since I was a small guy, not a real imposing presence.

But damn if the Seals didn't give me another shot.

It was like an act of God – or a bad Hollywood movie, take your pick. I was like the baseball player who gets kicked out of the Major Leagues and kicks around in the Minors thinking he'll never find his way back, but then gets a miracle break. That's what it was like for me. Only problem was, after they had agreed to let me try again, I discovered to my horror the Seals had lost all of my hard-earned diving records! So I had to quickly do all of my diving tests again and pass – and then, to add another horror to the growing list, I had to take that dreaded math test again.

This time I passed.

Now, I was finally back where I had started, training with 130 other guys to make the final cut, praying that nothing went wrong for me, because, of course, the Navy Seals were incredibly selective. Just because they had allowed me to try again didn't mean my placement was a sure thing. Far from it.

And at this point, my confidence was almost shot. I had to keep it together while we dived and handled demolitions with other sailors next to me shooting automatic weapons. If I made one wrong move, if I hesitated or acted unsure, another candidate might single me out and say he didn't want to dive with me, he didn't think he'd be safe working with a loser like me. Or an instructor could catch me completely mishandling a weapon and kick me out in a split-second. And this time around, it would be for good, there would be no third chance for me.

But I didn't falter. I made it through the whole training. Out of the 130 guys, 16 graduated to become a Navy Seal. I'm proud to say I was one of those 16.

I spent five years as part of Seal Team 4. No, I didn't spend those years taking out terrorists in Afghanistan or Iraq. This was before all of those actions took place. No, I was part of the Caribbean Defense Force – which maybe doesn't sound like the most dangerous duty in the world, but, hey, somebody had to do it! Reagan was president at the time and our team was actually given high-priority assignments by his administration, given the problems that happened in Grenada at the time.

Entrepreneur to Coach to Thought Leader

Thanks to my elite military training, I left the service a better man than I went in. Perhaps the most important attributes I gained were a strong and committed mindset dedicated to accomplishing goals and the discipline to see challenges through.

Those qualities were what enabled me, with the help of a couple of other entrepreneurial pals, build a successful business from scratch, an environmental consulting firm for developers, builders and governments. I just used the same discipline I had in the military to make our new company grow; we slowly built it up by regularly meeting in a local Waffle House, simply because we didn't have an office space. We would all meet up on Wednesdays and work off of our laptops and cellphones, trying desperately not to get any syrup on anything – then we'd go on to our individual homes and finish our work there, as well as go to job sites to meet clients in the field.

Our eventual success was gratifying. We were able to buy our own property for the business – bad news for the Waffle House's revenues – and, for 20 years, we did very well with it. But at the same time, something else was pulling at me.

It started in the evenings, when I'd go to the climbing gym or workout gym, and people would see what I was doing and want to know more about me. They'd ask, "Where did you learn how to climb?" "I was in the military," I would answer, "The Navy Seals." "Wow – how does that work?" they wanted to know.

So I'd give them some details about the kind of elite training routines I learned, and pretty soon they'd be asking, "Would you mind coaching this group of athletes over here? I'll give you a free membership at this gym." Or, "Would you help coach the youth team? They've got a competition coming up."

My Navy Seal background gave me instant credibility, which counted for a lot when I talked to kids about discipline and accountability. I told them how I used to be like them, until I learned what to do with myself. What was maybe more inspiring to them was the fact that I didn't look like some kind of giant muscle bound Hollywood action star – that's how people think of Navy Seals. But I didn't fit that stereotype, and that made kids think, "Hey, if he could do all that, maybe I could do too..."

It all kind of snowballed. They kept asking me about my workout routines. I didn't want to have to keep repeating myself, so eventually, I wrote them down for people to use. That's when somebody suggested, "Hey – you should do a blog on this stuff." Sure – why not? If it would help people, I'd put in the time and spread the information.

Soon, I started getting a lot of hits – and also requests for certain kinds of info. People wanted to know what kind of protein powder I used or some recipes for healthy, tasty meals. So I posted about those subjects. And then I started monetizing the blog, just to see what would happen. I was surprised to discover one day, after adding up the money that was coming in, that I was making more from the blog than I was from people hiring me to coach at the gyms.

It was around five years ago that I finally made the leap and went full-time with my blogging and coaching. I was making good money and blogging and coaching directly tied in to my passion. I felt like I could help people and directly impact their lives in a positive way.

The Entrepreneurial Mindset

More and more, lately, my coaching has taken a turn towards helping entrepreneurs gain the mental toughness they need in today's rugged marketplace. So I share my own story and relate it to their struggles. I ask them, "How many of you have been laughed at? Or flat-out rejected? Or told you would never make it to the goal you want more than anything else?" Because I went through all those humiliations and more – including having my diving records trashed!

What I did ain't no different from anything entrepreneurs like those of you reading this are doing. The lifestyle of an entrepreneur can be just as challenging as a Navy Seal's. You constantly get up early and end up working late, because you gotta make things happen, even if it seems like Mission: Impossible. It's a tough road, and there's no real road map for each individual trying to find their way. People respect me for my service as a Navy Seal – but I respect entrepreneurs on the same level for digging in to do their own thing.

Like I said, I don't resemble the picture most people carry around in their head of what a Navy Seal should look like. So I get asked, "How did you pull that off?" My answer comes down to four little words that add up to a hugely important concept: *I did not quit.* Instead, I hung in there and grinded it out. And that's exactly what you have to do as an entrepreneur.

For most entrepreneurs, it's not about wearing $600 shoes or wearing a bespoke suit created for you in London. You don't have a private jet to fly you around on a whim. Instead, you're working 24/7 and a lot of the time, it's in your gym shorts and flip-flops, just trying to get everything done. It's not as glamourous as some people seem to think it is – but, then again, neither is being a Navy Seal -- if people really saw how dirty a job being a Seal is, they probably wouldn't want to do that either. You could be knocking down doors and killing dudes. You could be waiting in a mosquito-infested swamp just to see if a specific boat is coming in – and, six hours later, going crazy from boredom and awful discomfort. But you push through to do what you have to do.

An entrepreneur, too, has to push through. If you want a shot at having those $600 shoes and that private jet, you got to get through it and pay some major dues. *And you have to not quit, no matter what.* Believe me, when I was training with the Seals, I saw guys quit – a lot of them. Including ones who were 6'2" and completely physically intimidating. You think to yourself, "If that guy couldn't make it – how do I have a shot?"

The answer is, you always have a shot. As long as you stay in the game, you can win it. But if you bow out before the final score is posted, yeah, you're going to lose, but only because you *chose* to lose.

In conclusion, I'd like to challenge every entrepreneur reading this to focus on your "Why." *Why* did you decide you wanted to be an entrepreneur? I know why I wanted to become a Navy Seal – I wanted to do right by my family, earn their respect and, especially, make my dad proud of me. I kept keying into that "Why" throughout the pain and the relentless challenges and it helped me stay committed to the task in front of me, no matter how hard it was.

So identify your "Why." Remind yourself of it and cultivate it on a daily basis. That "Why" may change as you continue onward, but as long as it's within you and it's strong, it's going to keep you in the game all the way to the end.

Discovering My
Marketing Superpowers

By Janette Gleason

As any superhero fan knows, the origin story is very important to the myth. Whether it's Batman vowing vengeance after his parents are murdered or Iron Man creating his special armored suit after being captured by terrorists, there is always a defining moment where our hero digs deep and commits to a life mission that motivates him or her to achieve great things.

Well, the chapter you're about to read features one of the most compelling origin stories of any of our Marketing Avengers. Janette Gleason is a best-selling author, business coach, strategist, entrepreneur, small business owner, consultant, speaker, teacher and award-winning marketer – but she might never have discovered all those "super powers" if she hadn't gone through...well, read on and you'll see for yourself. Let's just say this is one Avenger who definitely doesn't quit!

- Richard Seppala

I WAS RAISED TO BE A traditional wife and mother – in the spirit of Donna Reed, *Leave It to Beaver* and all those other 1950's and 60's TV shows – and that's what I expected to be when I grew up. After all, that was how I was brought up. My brother and I were raised in a Chicago suburb by a stay-at-home mom and a working dad and I loved how our family functioned. Why wouldn't I want to duplicate what I considered to be perfection?

Of course, in the meantime, I still wanted to support myself and gain some useful skills, so I went to college with the aim of becoming a teacher. And I was lucky enough to get a job teaching elementary school right after I graduated. I still remember the time a couple of years later – this was the late '90's – when they put a computer in my classroom. I really embraced the new technology and, because I did take the time to learn how to use it, I soon found myself teaching the other teachers how to use PowerPoint and other programs to improve their teaching capabilities.

That was the first indication of my professional future beyond the classroom – because I found that I caught on fast when it came to the practical application of software to make life easier and learning more effective. When others were overwhelmed by the new technology, they came to me to find out how to make it work the way they wanted to. And I was happy to help.

Still, after several years of teaching, I was ready to fulfill what I felt was my true ambition – to be a part of that traditional household I wanted to emulate. I had met my husband Joe in college and we both agreed that's what we wanted for our family. So, after our second of three children was born, we decided I would become a stay-at-home mom – and we would move to Arizona. We sold our house, packed up everything we owned and invested everything into my husband's financial planning business.

There, everything would be perfect, right?

The Crash

Okay, you may have guessed by that two-word subheading that maybe it wasn't all that perfect. At first it was, though. I did help out with Joe's business here and there, doing little things like payroll for instance, but mostly, I was all about being a mom to our small children.

Then came 2008.

I'm sure you remember that time, when the country hit financial bottom, the banks were freefalling and there was panic in the air. Well, businesses like Joe's were incredibly hard hit – nobody wanted to make a move with their finances until things calmed down, and nobody was sure when that would happen. We, like many others, were suddenly upside down with our own finances.

There we were with three kids, ages 6, 4, and 2 – and we couldn't pay our mortgage. We had to deal with foreclosure, bankruptcy – and we even had cars repossessed. I remember when we really hit rock bottom - that was the day I had to drop off the two older kids at school and I had no lunch I could send with them. We literally had nothing more in the house. I had to ask the teacher to please make sure they had something to eat that day and thankfully, she did.

It was the kind of moment where you ask, "What *else* can go wrong?" And lo and behold, something else did go wrong – Joe's office manager quit right before the holidays. I'm sure she saw where things were going – and went to find a safe job somewhere else. But for us, it felt like another death blow.

Rebirth

I really had no choice.

For Joe's business to keep running, I had to come in and help him run the office – and find a replacement for the person who left. So I did. I answered phone calls, greeted his clients, went through the mail and took care of everything else while we started the interview process.

But while I was running the office, I happened to take a good hard look at Infusionsoft, the automated CRM software system that Joe had been using for a couple of years. Again, the technology behind it fascinated me – and I started tinkering around with it, getting to know its capabilities. I would ask Joe, "Did you know it could do this? Or this? Or this?" And, of course, he didn't know what all it could do, he was busy focusing on his clients' needs, not the software system.

Me? I had the time to delve deep into what this thing could do. I started watching tutorials, checking out webinars and figuring again how to practically apply its features to our marketing needs – it was just like figuring out how to use PowerPoint at my elementary school all over again. And it was exciting for me, because we already had the system in place, we already had the names of plenty of clients that loved working with Joe – as well as the names of a lot of prospects we had been gathering over the years. To me, this was a godsend. To me, this could be the resource we needed to get out of the mess we were in.

I fell in love with marketing and with Infusionsoft.

People laugh at me when I say that, but it was true – because it was the beginning of our turnaround. This dark time had somehow brought out the best in me – I wasn't looking to acquire this skill, but suddenly I found I was a whiz at creating marketing campaigns that worked. For example, we had a tax preparation portion of our business – and by promoting it through Infusionsoft, we helped double our revenue that year, which helped us invest back in the financial planning side of the company.

An Unexpected Career

Our finances were on the upswing – and so was my confidence in myself. When I saw an advertisement for the Infusionsoft Ultimate Marketer contest, I said to myself, "Well, hey, that could be me!" And I ended up being selected as one of their finalists – and winning a brand new red Camaro to boot!

As a result, I was suddenly perceived as a marketing expert and ended up speaking in front of a few thousand people. Just a few months ago, I had been a stay-at-home mom worried to death about going broke and now, here I was, telling other people how I had marketed our business back to health? I never expected this – or expected that other people would be approaching me to help them like I helped Joe. I wasn't ready for that kind of invitation, and at first, I would just say, "It's just a hobby, I like to do it, I'm not a professional." But then consulting with others turned into regular part-time work and then, as all the kids began going to school, it became more like a fulltime career.

My newfound superpowers had saved the day. In addition to Joe regaining success, I now had my own business as well. I put together a team and kept on growing – intent on using those superpowers for the good of all my new clients! Today, those clients include small business owners, as well as leaders and executives at large organizations.

On the small business front, I help a lot of service professionals who know how I helped Joe – and want me to work that kind of marketing magic with their practices. These are people who, like Joe, want to serve their current clients as well as possible, in addition to getting referrals and new prospects in the door. I advise them on all that and help them to automate their internal processes – by using different technologies to run their businesses with less staff.

I also love to help authors, speakers and coaches because of my own teaching background. One thing I specialize in is taking their content, perhaps that keynote speech they've been giving that works like gangbusters, and creating a powerful online information product from it, such as a video or audio program or a chapter in a book (like this one!).

As I've mentioned, I also have a lot to offer larger organizations as well. Very often, they have content that they want to get out to all their members in a mass-produced manner – but they just don't know how to create the right systems to make that happen. That's where I come in, with the help of Infusionsoft. I can coach and train everyone on how to create the systems (that's where my teaching background really comes in handy) – or I can create the program myself for them to use.

My Superpowers

My new career has taught me a lot about myself that I didn't know – including identifying the "superpowers" I possess that, luckily, my clients really appreciate. Here are the special abilities I always put to work whenever someone hires me:

Laser-beam Focus

I am really super-focused – which causes me to dig hard until I have a very clear idea of where I'm going or what I want something to look like even before I've begun a job. In turn, that helps me guide clients through strategic planning and get very detailed about asking things like, "If we fast-forward one year from now, what would success look like?" Once we understand what we want our destination to look like, then I work together with the client to create a solid plan to get there.

My high level of focus also guides me when I'm researching. If I'm creating a training program for a client, I instantly start researching other programs similar to the one my client wants, so I can see for myself what works – and what doesn't. Then I can pull out the best features out of those programs and make sure they're a part of the one I'm building.

Making the Complex Simple

Everyone gets overwhelmed by certain tasks, especially if those tasks involve technology they're unfamiliar with. As I mentioned, my husband Joe simply didn't have time to deal with Infusionsoft's many features, because he was too busy trying to run his business. A lot of my clients are in the same position – they have plenty of skills and talents in their specific fields, but they don't have the space to learn how to create marketing campaigns that will reach the audience they're after.

Fortunately, I'm able to make those kinds of things easy for them to handle, so they can use these systems without being intimidated by what they *don't* know. I compare it to me using an iPhone – I have no idea what's inside the device that makes it work, I just know what button to push or which way to swipe on the screen to do specific tasks. That's how easy I want to make it for my clients. They don't need to know the coding that goes into an Infusionsoft campaign, they just need to know how to use it. I'm able to make that process simple for them and make them feel okay about working with it.

Even if they have problems, I'm a phone call away to guide them through them.

Internal GPS

When you take a road trip to somewhere you've never been before, you use a GPS system to get you there, right? Well, I have a great internal GPS (thanks to my focusing skills) – so that once the client and I set a group of goals, I can calculate the best route to achieving them. Yes, there will be obstacles and detours along the way – but that's when we recalculate and find our way around those difficulties.

Identifying Blind Spots

If you run your own business, you know how easy it is to get too close to a project or even your overall business objectives – and lose your way. Because you're so invested in outcomes, you sometimes don't see what you need to see – and, as a result, you develop blind spots.

As a consultant and coach, I'm good at helping people find those blind spots – but that's because I'm on the outside looking in. You can see a lot more when you're studying a process as an observer than you can when you're in the middle of developing that process – and, frankly, that's a big part of my value to my clients.

By the way, I develop my own blind spots too - I'm human and I fall into the same traps. That's why I hire coaches and consultants as well, so they can take a look at the big picture for me and help me correct blind spots that I've missed.

It's so important to do that. Why? Because once we identify a weakness or a problem, we can then begin to make plans to address it and we can experience more success in our businesses and our daily lives.

Automating Businesses

My technology expertise allows me to created automated systems that help any business run smoother, more affordably and more efficiently. Whether it's an Infusionsoft campaign or project management software, there are many technologies I can introduce to a client that will make his or her business life better. When you can make great things happen with a push of a button, isn't that worth investing in? I've found it definitely is!

While I enjoy flying into action as a "Marketing Avenger," I also still love my "secret identity" as a wife and mom – my original ambition in life. Every day, I make the kids pancakes or waffles, drive them to the school in the family minivan, and, whenever I can, I nurture and encourage their dreams.

But – there comes a time when the kids are at school, when my "hotline" rings – and on the other end is a business owner in distress. They might say, "I have Infusionsoft and I don't know how to use it!" Or "I have all these ideas that I don't know how to put into action!" I always reassure them that help is here and it's okay. And then I roll up my sleeves and go to work for them.

That's when I feel like I'm switching out the mini-van for the Red Camaro I won in the marketing contest. Because picturing that Camaro reminds me of all the hard work I did to earn it. Throughout this journey over the past few years, I've discovered a confidence and leadership ability within myself that I had no idea was there. And it's exciting when I realize I know what people need better than they know what they need – and can give them the answers, the guidance or the ideas to help them get to where they want to go. And it's not just me that's there to help them. I have a communications manager, a campaign strategist, a virtual assistant and a graphic designer, a full-blown virtual team to back me up whenever I need them.

I've been told by my coaches and clients that my mothering experience definitely spills over into my professional life. Often, I get called the "Queen Bee," because I want to make sure every one of my clients is doing great – and if they're not, I want to do what it takes until they are. So I think I'll take that as my Marketing Avenger name!

Finally, what's really wonderful is knowing how many other potential Marketing Avengers are out there to be discovered. One of my great clients and friends, Lisa McQueen, saw me speak at Infusionsoft, after I had placed as a finalist in the contest. She hired me for her and her husband's business and they experienced massive success – because, like me, Lisa took to the technology like a duck to water. I encouraged her to enter the Ultimate Marketer Contest like I had and coached her through the process.

Well, the student eclipsed the teacher – and Lisa became the Grand Prize Winner. That's the kind of awesome accomplishment a Queen Bee loves to see come out of her hive – and I'm anxious to see what other success stories lie in my future.

Accelerate Your Success!

By Ed O'Keefe

When it comes to super-powered marketers, there are few more successful than Ed O'Keefe. Many of you know his name from his former Dentist Profits coaching group; now Ed is focusing on his new Marine Essentials supplements line, which brings its customers the latest cutting-edge natural ingredients to tackle a variety of health and aging issues. Whatever the endeavor, you can bet on Ed realizing mighty results – because this is one Marketing Avenger who's got the goods!

Ed is now finishing up a new potential bestseller entitled Time Collapsing, where he shares his exclusive advice on how to make it to the top of your field a whole lot faster than your competition. And he should know – he first experienced massive success while in his twenties! In this chapter, he provides a sneak peek with some great tips on how to find shortcuts to marketing success.

- Richard Seppala

WE'RE ALL TAUGHT TO WAIT FOR OUR TURN.

As kids, we're told you go through the various grades of school, advance and eventually graduate. If we want a good job, we go to college. If we want to get promoted and make real money, we have to be patient and wait for a higher position to open up. That's traditionally the American Way – and the way of most of the world, for that matter.

Yeah, that's what we're taught.

But what if there are ways to take significant shortcuts to the top of your professional class? Shortcuts that work – and take you from obscurity to being a leading innovator and/or earner in your field? What if you didn't have to wait to take your turn?

What if you "jumped line" – and made it be your turn *now*?

Let's talk about how to make that happen.

Collapsing Time

If you're a marketer, you want the fastest results possible – both for your own business efforts and for your own future path to success.

I was no different when I first started out, even though it took me a while to lock into what I wanted to do with my life. In college, I was an athlete, playing on the volleyball team, and I also studied nursing. But then I decided nursing was not what I wanted to do with my life; what I really wanted to be was an entrepreneur. But I had no idea how to make that happen for me.

So, from the ages of 23 to 26, I struggled. I was broke and desperately wanted to change my circumstances – so I took control and began training myself for success. I went from seminar to seminar to seminar, getting my own personally-selected education in such marketing disciplines as NLP programming and hypnosis - while, at the same time, getting schooled in accelerated learning techniques so I could master these disciplines quickly. My own athletic experience allowed me to practice these techniques by coaching other athletes, as well as running seminars of my own and doing a lot of speaking engagements. This, in turn, quickly made me an expert in these areas; I was excited about how fast I mastered them.

More importantly, working with high-performing athletes, I saw for myself how they were able to push themselves to go from zero to sixty without taking a breath. I saw how they used certain core distinctions to jump ahead of their competition and make their mark immediately. That's the experience I aimed to replicate, but in the marketing and entrepreneurial space.

Then came my real breakthrough – direct response marketing. Once I discovered you could combine that technique with the compelling attraction of solving a problem or providing a needed service – well, I was off to the races. I studied those systems, using my new quick-learning techniques, and put them to work.

That resulted in my first entrepreneurial efforts, when I became a marketing coach to dental practices. At first, I had zero experience in this area. However, I had licensed the rights to a product, a product which gave me an instant position as an authority. Between that and the learning I had mastered, I suddenly found myself within 18 to 24 months running the largest dental marketing coaching group around - at the age of 26!

Start at the Top!

I accomplished all this early success thanks to uncovering one simple secret – You should always defy the traditional limits ingrained in us when we're little kids!

It's what I call sequential thinking, or the stepladder mentality – what I described at the beginning of this chapter. It starts when we progress from preschool to elementary school, from middle school to high school, then college and out into the working world in the area we studied. We're taught there's a progression we all *must* follow in order to get to where we want to go.

And it's simply not true.

Here's an interesting statistic: 83% of the population ends up in a different profession or occupation that what they studied in college. And I'm sure if you asked the average person if they were taught skills in school they would need in the real world to acquire wealth, they'd answer no. That's why 76% of working-age people are living paycheck-to-paycheck (and that number includes some high-earners, by the way).

The "traditional path" to adulthood is filled with traps that cause people to attain very, very limited amounts of success in their working lives - or to even *fail* miserably. I've found the assumptions baked into our culture about how you "get to the top" just aren't valid – and that's why I am sold on the notion of "time collapsing," or subverting the usual stepladder mentality, so we all can experience success in a faster and more reliable way.

Here's the real story: When you kick over that stepladder and leap right to the top, you've got a much better chance of being financially rewarded for it. How is that possible? The answers are actually pretty simple.

1) **There's less competition at the top.** It's just you and the "big dogs," and they're not worried about you because they've already made it!

2) **The people who can actually help you are already at the top.** Once you're in the same rarified atmosphere as them, you have more access to them – and many of them are happy to mentor you or become a part of your operation.

3) **The knowledge and strategies you need are at the top.** And they'll help you accelerate growth in your business or personal life and attain whatever you're out to achieve.

The only way to learn how to be at the top, in my opinion, is to skip all the lower steps and soak up everything you can learn from others who have become masters at their expertise.

Now, let's drill a little deeper and uncover more about how you reach that top level with your marketing efforts.

How I Did It - How You Can Do It

Here are a few of the strategies I believe are crucial to taking your place at the peak of the top of the marketing mountain.

First of all, **understand what's possible in today's world.** What do I mean by that? Well, when I started my two hugely successful companies, both the dental coaching and the supplement business, *social media did not exist.* Now, it does – and in many forms, all of which have their distinct advantages when it comes to marketing a product or service. That means our ability to gain access to potential customers and to deliver a solution to their problems instantly has never been greater. Keep that in mind when you create your next campaign and match that campaign to the social media platform that most suits it.

Second, **lead with authority**. As I already shared, I bought the rights to an existing product when I began my dental coaching business; that product had a trust factor already built in that opened a lot of doors for me that ordinarily would have stayed locked shut. I used this approach again with my supplement business. I hired a doctor who had a lot of experience, not to mention a great deal of knowledge, when it came to anti-aging products, and we leveraged this experience and knowledge to help create our products and market them. I was certainly no expert when I started this business – so I hired somebody with credibility (the word "doctor" before his name helped!) who *was* an expert.

On the marketing side, I hired a top consultant who had been involved in supervising the sending of millions of direct marketing pieces in the supplement arena. From the get-go, she was running my campaigns, because she knew what she was doing and I was still getting up to speed.

Remember, in marketing, you don't have to position yourself as the expert. You can hire someone to serve in that role. Behind the scenes, it's the same deal. Get the people who have already done what you're trying to do. It's part of how you "collapse time." If you didn't hire people with this level of expertise, you'd have to spend a lot of time trying to achieve that level of experiential wisdom and knowledge yourself. With my approach, however, the only question you have to answer is, "Where do I get the money to hire these people?" – and make that happen.

And, for myself, I do firmly believe in spending the money to hire them and not taking on partners. I like having the flexibility to control my own time and personal lifestyle choices – maybe it's because

I have seven kids ranging from ages 2 to 11! You might be different and you might thrive in a partnership arrangement – that works if you can make it work, **you just have to know yourself.**

What do I mean by that? Well, if you want to be a Marketing Avenger, it just makes sense that you have to understand what your own personal superpower is. It takes a while to understand what you're good at and how you like to put things together; it took me a couple of years, as I've already pointed out. There are tests you can take to delve more deeply into what your personality is all about, but I believe life experience and a lot of practical trial-and-error approaches is the best and fastest way to discover what you like – and what you don't like.

Next, **identify a good model (or models) you can base your marketing strategy on.** Look at the top businesses that are doing what you want to do – businesses that have been very successful at it for one reason or another. Well...what are those reasons? I have a process I take people through, showing them how to model market research all the way to the core sales process – including optimizing personal and corporate behavior. Once you learn how other top performers succeed, you can emulate their template and make it your own.

Another key point of accelerating success is **removing friction points.** Often, we're not performing at our best levels due to factors we're not aware of – but those factors slow us down and keep us from succeeding at the rate we should.

When I coach high-performing pro athletes, I deal with this issue a lot. And there are usually two different parts in play.

Mental blockages

We all have unconscious patterns that can easily get in our way. You could have been taught by your parents at an early age that making money was somehow a dishonorable pursuit and the shame creeps into your views on your business. Or you could have a fear of failing ingrained deep in your psyche which causes you to avoid taking necessary chances. These are emotional issues that need to be identified and reckoned with, or they'll keep getting in your way.

Waning Passion

People have certain life cycles where they are really passionate about doing something, then, after they get good at it, they start to lose their enthusiasm: "Been there, done that." We all like to move on to the "next big thing," and sometimes, when we repeat ourselves, we don't feel it's all that exciting. That's when it's time to find ways to align your passion and core goals to your marketing and business strategies – and think differently about what you're trying to do.

Finally, a little advice courtesy of George Costanza from the old *Seinfeld* show: **Do the opposite.** In one episode, George decides that every single decision he's made in his life has been the wrong one – so he decides to do the complete *opposite* of everything his instincts tell him to do. Result? George ends up dating a beautiful girl and gets a dream job with the New York Yankees.

I'm not suggesting you take this idea to those kinds of extremes (although, if you do, I'd love to know how it turned out for you!), but what I do suggest is that, after you create a step-by-step key marketing plan, stop and think a moment: What is the *opposite* of every single step you've outlined in that plan?

For example, if part of your plan is to spend money on advertising, what's the flip side of that? Maybe you can create a new, viral-based referral environment that costs virtually nothing – and brings you similar results. Perhaps another part of your plan involves making the price of the product as high as possible so you make as much as possible on the first transaction. The opposite of that approach would be to give the product away for free – so you get the most customers and, therefore, a list of the most "hot" leads you can continue to market to down the line. The "opposite" approach often uncovers something completely different from the usual marketing gimmicks - and something infinitely more powerful.

To sum up, if it isn't obvious already, I believe it's important to challenge assumptions and turn them on their heads to see what comes out of it. Start at the bottom? Why? Why not instead take a direct trip to the top by immediately adopting their tactics and their expert players? Why not assume you're going to be one of the top players and go for the gold?

Let everybody else wait in line. *You* don't want to waste that kind of time.

Are you ready to "collapse time?" Are you ready to step on the gas - and accelerate your rate of success? Then rise to the top without waiting for an invitation – and take your place there without hesitation. I hope you'll seriously considering putting the tools I outlined in this chapter into action – and forget that fable about the Tortoise and the Hare! Slow and steady never wins the race – the fastest does!

Remove Your Mental Blocks to Success!

By Mark Yuzuik

So there I am, onstage in Las Vegas, playing some amazing guitar licks that had the crowd rocking the night away...

Okay, well, that's what was happening in my head. The reality was this: Yeah, I was onstage in Las Vegas all right, but I was only playing the air guitar. Not only that, the entire audience was laughing at me, because master hypnotist Mark Yuzuik had me and a whole lot of other audience members doing all sorts of crazy things!

Yes, Mark is our next Marketing Avenger and he's about to entrance you with his secrets regarding the power of the unconscious mind, secrets you can utilize to boost your personal marketing skills!

- Richard Seppala

I CAN MAKE PEOPLE BARK like a dog. Speak Martian. I can make people think that, if they dance with everything they've got, they have a shot at appearing on the *Ellen* talk show next week.

That's the kind of fun stuff I do in my stage show. Offstage, it's a little more serious. I help people improve their lives in substantial ways in my seminars. For example, I help people lose weight – and you wouldn't believe all the thanks I get in return. Overweight people who have failed with every diet in the world suddenly lose 10 pounds, 20 pounds, even 60 to a 100 pounds, because of my techniques. It's great to see that happen.

Whether I'm prompting people to do something silly like yelling "Who's Your Daddy?" during my act – or helping them do something incredibly meaningful like quit smoking in one of my seminars – it's through the same basic process. *I am removing mental blocks that prevent someone from doing what they would not do under normal life conditions – even if it's something they desperately <u>want</u> to do.*

We all have mental blocks that stop us from getting what we want out of life. We unknowingly deny ourselves the results we're looking for in business and in our personal lives, because of something lurking beneath the surface. In this chapter, I'm going to reveal a few of my hypnosis techniques, so you can understand more about those blocks – and how to overcome them.

The Secret Behind Hypnosis

I wasn't always a hypnotist – as a matter of fact, I was openly mocking of the whole idea of hypnosis. One day, however, I received a call that changed my life forever. It was my brother, inviting me to go along with him to a fair to see a hypnosis show.

My immediate reaction? "C'mon, you can't be serious!" And I continued to make every joke possible about what I thought was a phony act (I've gotten paid back for that, by the way, by people making the same jokes about me over the years!). I was convinced that these audiences were filled with plants, people hired to act goofy when the hypnotist told them to. I found it impossible to believe that anybody could give complete strangers outrageous commands and expect them to actually do what they were told to do.

But then, after the performance, I talked to the hypnotist himself and found out that his act was for real. More importantly, I found out WHY hypnosis worked.

That night, he explained to me that the human mind is made up of two parts – the conscious and the subconscious. Then he asked me, "Have you ever done anything in life where you know you wanted the result and you didn't follow through, even though you had the knowledge and motivation?"

"Yeah," I answered. It was true.

"That was because of a program in your subconscious."

"A program?"

"A program, like a computer program. Your subconscious mind doesn't analyze complicated situations; it takes everything *literally*. A certain situation will cause it to react by running a certain program that may cause you to stop working for something you want – because it's afraid of that objective, for some reason. That's why you have to know how to influence your subconscious mind, that's *really* what's making big decisions for you."

He could tell I was hooked, so he went on.

"It's not hard to hypnotize someone. It's a lot harder to wake people up from their daily habits and routines, where they do things they don't want to do and feel ways they don't want to feel – because they're prisoners of their subconscious."

I was blown away by this revelation – and I suddenly wanted more than anything else to be a hypnotist myself. So I arranged for a friend of mine to do an infomercial with the hypnotist and, in return, he agreed to personally train me. We ended up becoming best friends - and three years later, I was doing a stage show of my own.

That's when I started realizing that I could take the art of hypnosis to another level. What I was told about the subconscious blocking life progress still haunted me – and I wondered if I could help people change destructive behaviors and help them get better results, so that they *could* get what they really wanted out of life. So I began doing seminars, in which I helped people fix the cause of the problem, not the problem itself. Only by changing the subconscious could I create better results – everything else was just like putting a Band-Aid on a wound.

The Pattern of Restriction

So why exactly do people stop moving forward? What in the subconscious stops them from accomplishing what they want to accomplish?

It's called the Pattern of Restriction and I'll give you an example of how it works.

Let's say I'm an entrepreneur that wants to be successful. I go to a seminar, I get all pumped up and motivated and I feel ready to go. For the next couple of weeks, my activity is off the charts, I'm doing everything I need to do and a whole lot more, because I feel like an unstoppable force.

Except – boom. All of a sudden, this unstoppable force...stops. I feel like I've hit a wall that I can't blast past. But the wall is all in my head.

That's when I encounter the Pattern of Restriction.

The Pattern of Restriction is a belief system that sends out powerful signals that what you want is impossible for you to get. It throws waves of doubt your way, waves that knock you down and keep you down. And it comes from fear, fear generated by other negative events earlier in your life.

And suddenly, you're saying to yourself, "I can't do what it takes right now to get what I want." And you procrastinate – because that procrastination is actually meeting your subconscious needs at the moment. It's giving it benefits, believe it or not!

"How does procrastinating give me benefits?" you're probably asking. Simple. Because now you get to create a story that satisfies all that doubt and also gives you an excuse to stop trying. Your story might be, "I can't put all my energy into this new business now, I'm not spending enough time with my family." Or, "I can't invest any more time and money right now, I'm risking too much and it's gonna come back to haunt me."

Then after a while, you start questioning your own excuses and procrastination. "Dude, you're better than this," you say to yourself and you get yourself all pumped up again to take a second run at this.

And boom! Because that Pattern of Restriction is still in place, your subconscious causes you to hit another wall down the line.

That's when you start accommodating the doubt more and more. Is what you have right now all that bad? You're safe, you don't have to risk anything, why try so hard to make things better? So you stop again.

Rinse and repeat. This Pattern of Restriction can keep going forever and you can keep creating more and more stories in your conscious mind to stop yourself from your dreams – all to prevent any more anxiety from filling up in your subconscious.

What hypnosis does is that it finally breaks that pattern; it gets you to take the action you need to take and, at the same time, remove the fear and stop the procrastination. You get the results you want – and that in turn destroys the pattern of restriction.

Not only that, it empowers you to go for bigger goals!

Changing the Stories We Tell Ourselves

A lot of the time, reprogramming the subconscious and breaking Patterns of Restriction comes down to the stories we tell ourselves.

For example, I hold seminars for people who want to quit smoking. I ask the group – "Who wants to stop smoking?" Everybody raises their hands, of course, because that's why they're in the room. Then I ask, "Would you do whatever it took to be non-smokers?" They nod enthusiastically, but they also say things like, "I've tried everything and nothing works." Their Pattern of Restriction is already showing – because they're telling a story that already sets them up for failure with me.

So I pick somebody out of the group and ask, "Do you have kids?"

He answers in the affirmative.

"How old are they?" I ask.

He says, "Four and eight."

"Would you do anything for them?"

"Sure," he answers with emotion.

I pause – then ask, "Do they smoke?"

He laughs at the idea. I'm not laughing.

"Do you want them to smoke?" I ask seriously.

Now he's serious again. "No."

"Well," I say, "You're the biggest influence on them and they're going to mirror and match your behavior. So they will probably smoke for that reason. Have you tried to stop smoking for your kids before?"

He answers, "Yeah, I have." I know that's going to be his answer. I'm setting him up for what's coming next.

"When do you smoke?"

"When I'm drinking and hanging out with friends."

"When else?"

"When I'm stressed."

"When else?"

"Um...all the time."

"Why do you want to quit smoking?"

"Because I hate it."

"Obviously you don't, everything you do with cigarettes indicates they're your best friends. They get rid of stress, they make hanging out more enjoyable..."

"I hate it."

"Why?"

"Because it costs a lot of money, it's bad for my health, it stinks..."

At this point, he's listing logical reasons he wants to stop smoking. But there's no emotion behind those reasons, like there is for the reasons he likes to smoke. Smoking meets his emotional needs – and my chance of getting him to quit are slim to none.

Unless I get him to change the story of what cigarettes mean to him.

Now, to do that, I have to have the right leverage. Right now, smoking to him is based on pleasure – and quitting means a negative, a loss in his life. That's why he can't stop. I have to change that subconscious story.

Next, I simply ask, "If I were to give you a check for $100,000 to stop smoking for 90 days, would you do it?"

"Yeah!" he answers with such enthusiasm.

To him, money will solve problems and give him more pleasure than smoking would. That's why he's excited about the idea. He can improve his lifestyle, buy anything he wants, get more attention from people...all of that great, positive stuff is buried in his subconscious, which is silently cheering him on. That's why he doesn't have to think about his answer.

I say, "Well, that's interesting. You'll quit for $100,000, but you won't quit for your kids."

And with that sentence, I own him.

"Earlier, you told me you would do anything for your kids because you love them so much," I continue. "Now, I believe you love them - but you just said you can't quit for them, but you can for money. Do you care more about money than your kids? Think about it. I'm not going to tell you have to quit – as a matter of fact, you can smoke as much as you want. But what I think you should do from now on is smoke in your house, in your bathroom. And bring your four-year-old and your eight-year-old into that bathroom when you do it. As a matter of fact, I want you to pull out three cigarettes right now."

I wait for him to pull out the three cigs.

"When you smoke, "I go on, "you should put one cigarette in your mouth and one in each of theirs. Light all three and blow smoke in each other's faces...if you ask them to do it, they'll do it, because they want to please their father. They would harm themselves to show their love for you."

What I'm doing with all this is taking away the pleasure from the cigarettes – instead, I'm linking them to massive pain, the pain of physically harming their kids. And I make them hold the cigarettes when I tell them all this, so they have a tactile connection to what I'm saying at the same time they visualize it. I'm using *three* modes of communication to plant this image.

And finally I say, "Feel that situation in your heart. Imagine what it's going to be like."

Many times at this point, they just tear up. Whoever is watching tears up, because they can relate to it. And about 90% of the time after that, the person I do this with will become a nonsmoker from that moment on. Because I just put a new story into their subconscious, a new story that says cigarettes mean harm to their children and if they don't stop, they don't really love them.

Cigarettes are no longer their best buddies.

Unleashing Your Inner Entrepreneur

This is the kind of technique that works with all sorts of life issues – drinking, obesity and even marketing. Yes, that kind of hypnotic technique can help you sell and market yourself and your products at a much higher level. It's a matter of creating a new program in the subconscious mind, a program that says, "You should think like a multimillionaire, you should do what multimillionaires do - look for opportunity, take action when you see it, and move forward." It's about removing fear and doubt, and taking yourself from frustration to achievement.

For example, let's say you have a three-day event scheduled. You want to motivate the people who show up, you want to sell them on you and your program and move them into a $40,000 coaching program at the end of the event, a program that's going to help them grow their business exponentially.

Well, it could be you have a Pattern of Restriction that might prevent you from gaining everything you could out of an event like this. You might hesitate or lose faith that anyone is actually going to buy into the coaching program – and the crowd will sense that lack of confidence in how you present that program.

That's where someone like me comes in. I can demonstrate to you how you can train your unconscious to break out of the negative program in your subconscious and empower you to give it all you've got – for real. Again, it's not about you not having the know-how or experience to convert your seminar attendees into your coaching program, it's about you breaking free of anything inside your mind that might be holding you back.

A hypnotist can actually be the insurance policy to make sure you succeed, so you can eliminate fears, get rid of any hesitations and help your leads take action on what they already want to take action on. They wouldn't be at your seminar if they weren't interested in taking the next step – they're already motivated. I can help you move them to the next step, because they are already invested in what you're selling.

As I tell you this, I want to correct one big misconception about this kind of hypnosis technique: It's not about the subject waking up and suddenly being crazy-motivated to do something. What I do only works if you already have the motivation to do it – the hypnosis only allows you to take action from a secure place without any fear. When you reach that place, the results can indeed be spectacular. I had one person text me a couple of weeks after one of my seminars that he made $115,000 based on the principles I taught him – because he got past a major mental block and was able to put in the maximum effort for the first time in his life.

The success, like everything else I do, is measurable.

I invite you to contact me if I can be of any help with your business.

Scale to Grow!

By Vinnie Fisher

If I had to guess who Vinnie Fisher's favorite superhero was, I'd say Giant-Man – because that guy can grow and grow on demand!

Well, that's Vinnie's approach to business in general; if there's a way to make it grow, he'll find it, just as he's done with his own super-successful companies over the years. For him, "Super-Size" isn't just something you ask the local McDonalds to do with your order, it's something you do with your revenues and your service to your customers. That in turn adds a special extra something to your marketing efforts, because people know it's backed by a team that's scaled to grow and built to serve them.

In this chapter, Vinnie's going to give away some of his biggest secrets to making that happen, by putting together the most effective group of employees, a group that shares your vision for growth and knows how to bring it to life.

- Richard Seppala

STARTING A COMPANY can seem so simple. You create a viable product or service and then determine an effective sales message to generate orders. The money starts coming in and you're in business.

Easy as pie, right?

Sure, at that moment it is – because that's the moment when your company can provide its greatest level of service at the cheapest cost of delivery. But that moment passes quickly and things have to change. You can't grow a business properly if you're going to try and do everything yourself – and that means you have to begin hiring people to really transform your company into a moneymaking powerhouse.

And that's when things get really interesting.

Almost every client of mine has major issues hiring the right employees to be on their team. People being people, those issues spring from a variety of factors, but the biggest reason in my opinion? It's because *most business owners are not experts on hiring.* They just don't understand that the most important key to operating a successful company is having the *right* people serving in the *right* roles.

The hiring process should not be a guessing game. In fact, there should be no guesswork involved at all. I've conducted thousands of interviews and employed over 1,600 employees during my career – so I've learned a lot of hard and important lessons. Let me share a few of them in this chapter.

Core Values

Frequently, a hiring process begins and ends with verifying if the candidate can do the job that's required of them: Do they have the necessary skills and talents, and do they seem to be a good worker? If the business owner feels those questions are answered to their satisfaction, then fine. They're hired.

Of course having the right skills is important, but what can be just as critical is if the person shares your *core values.* Personnel issues typically stem from the fact that we often hire for competence instead of culture.

One time, we were looking for someone to join our programming team. I met with one young man and watched as he easily passed our competency-programming test. Then he passed our first interview with flying colors. I started to get real excited about his skills, so excited that I didn't spend any time looking into any red flags or issues that he may have had. We offered him the job and he took it. And then the wheels fell off almost immediately after he started.

His lack of commitment to the job started to show right away. He was often late, sloppy in his code, and short with fellow team members. Within a few weeks, we had no choice but to fire him. After reevaluating our process, we decided he should never have been hired in the first place.

Which taught me this lesson: *In order to acquire good team members, you need to have a gauge with which to properly evaluate people.*

My gauge is determining if they match our core values. If you don't already have your core values in place, I recommend the following process:

1. Write down between 10-15 one-word values that describe you and your executive team (if you have one).
2. Narrow this list down to the five you feel most strongly about and have your team do the same.
3. Meet with the executive team and have each person state their five values and why they selected them.
4. Determine the five you all can strongly agree on and use them as your company's five core values.

Not too long ago, I did this exercise with the executive team at my company, Fully Accountable™. I could have predicted what would happen – we ended up lining up on all *five* of our core values: Competence, Confidence, Caring, Honesty and Commitment. That made for a great day, filled with lots of energy and vision as we defined the things that mattered most and found ways to implement them within the company.

Since then, we discovered that if an employee shares at least three of these five values, their success rate with us goes through the roof. When they only share one or two, it usually doesn't work out. And that's how we discovered the absolute importance of this criteria.

Hiring Your Key People

As an entrepreneur, it's up to you to decide what roles you want to fill in your company; but it's also a case where too much freedom can do you in. Earlier in my career, I made the mistake of hiring people exactly like myself, because I wanted someone who would get things done the way I did. The reality was, however, I needed to create a team of people *who could perform tasks I was not good at doing*. I really didn't need another "me." If I was good at accounting, why would I go after another person who was good at accounting at an early stage of my business? Better I had somebody who was better at customer service or office organization.

That's why, before you start hiring, you should make an assessment of what you actually need out of a new employee, some part of the business that you either can't or don't want to fill yourself. That way, both of you can focus on your individual strengths to deliver the best for your company. You can't execute as a team unless you have the right people focusing on the right details.

Personally, I would never start a company with less than three people. Sometimes you may not have the resources to do that, but ideally, you should have the following three key roles in place:

Entrepreneur/Creator: This person is usually the owner or founder of the company, but not always. They should be working on the acquisition of revenue, not on the completion of tasks.

Technician: Someone has to deal with the actual nuts and bolts of the technology necessary to your company's success. I used to believe that you need to have all your technicians in your office, but times change and nowadays, technicians can be anywhere, including halfway across the globe. But they still need proper direction - which brings us to our third key role...

Manager: A manager keeps things running and is there to serve the entrepreneur and the technician by making sure all three parts of the business are integrated and working well together. The manager is in control of the implementation of the company's vision.

Starting out with this kind of three-pronged team makes success much more likely. It's extremely hard to do it alone with no one to collaborate with. Many investors refuse to put money into single-founder companies for that very reason. When you're a solopreneur, you have no safety net; if you stop working, there is no business. When you have an executive team, however, you have back-up, other skillsets and other perspectives.

The Right People Doing the Right Things: Project and Process People

In a work environment, to me, there are two types of people: You are either a *project* person or a *process* person. Let me explain what each of those terms mean.

Project People

A project person likes to take on new initiatives. They may not come up with the direction or vision for such an initiative, but they can take charge of completing it. However, once done, they won't be excited to do the same kind of project again, they always want to go on to the next thing. To a project person, repeating a task they've already done is about as exciting as watching paint dry.

Project people thrive in sales because they don't sell someone the exact same way every time. Marketing people are also more project-oriented because they need to change and craft their message constantly. Writers, typically creative writers and copywriters, also have more project-based mindsets, because they deal with a new subject every time.

Businesses frequently misuse project people. They think because the person was so good at a certain thing, they can repeat the same trick forty or fifty times – but that only results in that person losing interest and fizzling out in terms of their effectiveness.

Process People

A process person rarely likes generating an original idea and isn't comfortable being the one figuring how to accomplish something that hasn't been done before. However, if you hand them an action outline with 27 steps, not only will that outline grow to 35 steps, it'll be much improved.

A process person's complete joy in life is to do the same tasks over and over, and do them more efficiently each time. To a process person, being an innovator or a creator is so overwhelming that they shut down. To them, doing the same tasks on a daily basis, while finding ways to improve on them, is the only kind of innovation they're comfortable with.

Now – can you be both a project person AND a process person? I think so. Actually, I *know* so because we have one in our office: Rachel! She's an amazing person who can come up with ideas, but she does not want to be the one who creates the big picture. She falls short of vision, but the second she sees the goal, she can grab the ball quickly and run with it. She also isn't crazy about doing the exact same thing every day, which is why she's somewhere in the middle of process and project-oriented. What we have to do is make sure we've given her enough of the vision so that she can execute comfortably, while also helping her avoid doing the exact same tasks every day.

Want to know what kind of person a new hire happens to be? Just ask them, "Are you a project person or are you a process person?" Since they probably haven't heard those terms before, you may have to elaborate and ask, "Do you like to come up with ideas or do you like to take someone else's idea and make it better?" You'll be amazed at the results you get from this simple step.

So try to identify which kind of person your employees are and manage them to their specific mindset. You'll have a happier and much more productive workplace as a result.

The Triangle Offense

Just as there are three key people that are essential to a start-up, there are also three key attributes that every amazing employee possesses: Attitude, effort, and ability. When you can develop this winning trio to its fullest, you will have in place an unstoppable "Triangle Offense."

Let's examine each one in turn.

Attitude

People come in with the attitude that they have. They'll be exactly who they are and, depending on the environment, they're either going to thrive or not. This is why it is so essential that their character and values align with the mission and core values of the company. Our job is not to force them into our environment because they have an in-demand skill - our job is to make sure they are the right fit for our culture, because that's the only way their talent is going to shine.

Effort

If someone isn't willing to try hard and give something their all, they will not be successful. You want your workers to put in a 100% effort naturally, so you can trust them to do their work. You also want people who put in effort for *results,* not credit.

Ability

A potential hire has to have the skillset to be able to do the job. There are many cases where people can pick up the needed skills and eventually become proficient at them, but pre-qualified individuals will better meet the needs of roles that require special expertise.

Good teams do not happen by accident. That's why, during the hiring process, be sure to remember the Triangle Offense: Attitude, effort and ability.

Now – another question for you. Of these three attributes, which is the most important?

Well, at my company, we hire for attitude, followed by effort and, lastly, ability. Ability is important, but it has nothing to do with competence. If you don't have the right attitude, or if you're not willing to put in the effort, it doesn't matter how capable you are at the job. When doing interviews, we completely stop moving forward with an applicant if we find that their attitude doesn't fit with our company.

Management and the Triangle Offense

Attitude, effort, and ability also matter for managers – but in slightly different ways. A classic mistake that a lot of business owners make is to take their most competent person and throw them into a managerial role. The owner thinks, "Well, of course they should manage people! They're best at getting stuff done!" And they're wrong. In reality, being a good manager requires a very specific skillset. Let's look at how our Triangle Offense should apply to potential leadership roles:

When it comes to **attitude**, a true manager should always be looking for what's not getting done – and, if need be, get it done themselves. When I was in college, I had very little or no financial support from my family. That's not whining, it was just reality. So, in addition to taking out loans, I did all kinds of odd jobs, including one at a restaurant. There, I quickly moved from a server's role to house manager.

Why? I had the right attitude. If a table needed clearing and it wasn't in my section, I wouldn't look around to see whose job it was, I would just do it. If the dishwasher called off sick, guess who was washing dishes? If we needed to clean the bathrooms and everyone was busy, well guess what? "That's not my job" was not in my vocabulary and it shouldn't be in any manager's.

If there's one place where **effort** is needed the most, it's in a manager's role. As I noted, at the restaurant, I was willing to do everything no matter what my official title was at the time. Everyone, including the managers, had to be able to serve at the lowest level and be willing to put in the effort.

When you are a manager, your job is about serving the team to make sure that they get their jobs done correctly. And you are the person entrusted to remove barriers holding the team back from peak performance. One of my dearest friends says to those within his organization, "If service is beneath you, then leadership will always be above you."

Moving on, a manager's key **ability** has to be flexibility. Think of politics: Someone who is extremely right or left wing is stuck to their beliefs - they're not willing to change them no matter what the facts dictate. Well, a manager always must be a "moderate" – willing to change positions as long as they can stay within the bounds of certain core principles. You must be able to change and pivot in an organization – that's why we look for someone with the ability to be quick on their feet. At our company, Fully Accountable™, we all know we constantly have to flex and bend with the situation – and that example has to start at the top!

This is just a sampling of the kind of expertise any entrepreneur must apply to their hiring process. A huge part of your company's marketing appeal to any customer or client is how great your team serves them. And that's why any company that plans on growing to the next level must make sure they have the right people in the right roles. You don't have to hunt endlessly for some kind of magical unicorn to fill an important slot in your business. Instead, follow the proven steps of hiring and training I've shared here (and check out my new book, *The CEO's Mindset: How to Break Through to the Next Level* for more advice along these lines) - and you'll be well on your way to assembling and growing a world-class team!

Power Up Your People!

By Gayle Abbott and Elizabeth Weihmiller

Part of being a marketing superhero is having the right mindset. If Captain America, when he needs to throw a shield to stop an opponent, suddenly questions his ability to throw that shield accurately – well, he will probably hesitate and either throw the shield too late or miss the target all together!

That's where Gayle and Elizabeth come to the rescue. I call them the "Mindset Maximizers" – and in this chapter, they'll discuss how every business needs to focus on its people first!

- Richard Seppala

LET'S SAY YOU GREW UP TO BE A SUPER SALESPERSON.

You're known for closing the most difficult cases and you've risen to the top of your profession as a result. But suddenly something about what you're doing for a living is eating at your insides. You feel a little less motivated and a little less like doing your job. You begin to slip-up on returning messages and calls. Your figures go down. Something's wrong with your attitude and you have no idea what it could possibly be.

But maybe, when you were four years old, you were at the mall with your mom. Maybe an aggressive salesclerk worked hard to sell your mom something she either didn't want or couldn't afford. Maybe that salesclerk didn't stop until your mom was actually forced to rudely cut her off and get you away from that store as fast as you can.

And maybe when you asked, "What's the matter, Mommy?", she answered, "Salespeople. They're such slimy horrible people."

And maybe that remark just happened to stick in your head all these years – until it finally caused you to start shutting down the very talent that's responsible for your success.

Too often, when assessing ourselves and our co-workers, we focus on superficial behaviors and ignore the causes of those behaviors. Subconscious seeds of defeat can be planted at a very early age – and ultimately end up short-circuiting confidence, limiting performance and bringing progress both personally and professional to a screeching halt.

For over two decades, our company, Strategic Partners Alliance, Inc., has been helping entrepreneurs, CEOs and high-ranking executives in a wide range of companies both big and small power up their people skills so they and their staff can truly be the best to they can be. Our aim is to facilitate change and create a culture of performance that can move your company to world-class success, in terms of how our clients define that success – by blending practical techniques with intuitive and expert understanding of what makes people tick.

The People Problem

It seems almost common sense, but many forget that your success is mostly dependent on your people – and that includes you. They can be your greatest strength, but also your biggest challenge. That contradiction may seem daunting, but not to us. We're all about helping our clients dig deep to make positive change that allows them to gain the maximum ROI from both themselves and their employees.

What do we do differently from others in our business? We take a non-traditional and, we think, much more effective approach in assessing people (even though we're very familiar with those traditional approaches). 90% of assessments of management and employees focus on behavior to analyze how well people are going to perform. But that's like judging how good the food is at a restaurant by how nice its exterior is. It's a surface analysis that doesn't tell you what's really going on with someone – and how that might impact their performance in the future.

For example, many of us walk around with limiting beliefs about money. Psychologists have identified over 3000 of them, so the probability is high. For example, you may believe down deep inside that money is the root of all evil – or, perhaps, that you don't deserve to make a lot of it. When we do harbor one of these kinds of limiting thoughts, it will impact how we do business in a negative way at some point. But often, when we successfully identify and rid ourselves of these beliefs, the money starts flowing in because we are no longer sabotaging ourselves from being successful.

Then there are those who have a high level of worry and anxiety, a high level that creates a tense atmosphere and causes people to not want to engage with them. Because often that anxiety comes out in scolding and second-guessing those around them. No one enjoys being under needless scrutiny or getting that kind of pressure put on them every minute of the day.

Another quality that cause people to unknowingly disrupt their progress in business? Having a lack of confidence and believing they're not good enough to succeed. That often causes them to try too hard and never trust anything. They might reach a certain level of success, but then fail to do what they need to do in order to maintain it or grow it – because deep down, they feel like they aren't deserving of it.

Finally, another huge culprit in hindering performance is anger. Those who harbor rage at others and/or at themselves create a culture of criticism in which others stop being self-motivated and stop delivering. Tired of being attacked, co-workers merely wait to be told what to do so they won't be second-guessed - and, as a result, they don't perform as they should, which ends up hurting the business as a whole.

Moving Beyond Barriers to Success

So how does your business move beyond the negative beliefs and emotions we've described above?

Well, the first step is perhaps obvious – and that's doing some self-examination. You yourself may easily have one of these issues. That doesn't mean you're a bad person or you can't be successful, but it does mean you should take the time to understand yourself and look at what you may not be seeing. We all have compelling blind spots that cause us to put up barriers to success rather than empowering our own happiness and productivity. Being honest and brave enough to tackle your own negative beliefs and emotions makes a big statement to others – and also encourages them to do it themselves. It's the ultimate game of Follow the Leader.

But the second big challenge is making sure you get the *right* people in the jobs that you need to fill. That's why we'd like to share with you in this chapter what we consider to be the 5 Key Steps to Hiring Success, steps that will enable you to find people that will move you forward - rather than create a bottleneck of negativity that might block your own prosperity.

Key #1: Understand What Outcomes You Want

Many Human Resources departments will list a set of tasks in order to define an open position, when what an employer really needs to define is what the outcome of the job should be. If you want someone to come in and organize your office so that it runs more efficiently, *that* should be your goal, not to list the things a job applicant needs to do to organize the office. Anyone can do individual tasks, but not everyone can tackle the "big picture" outcome of a job – which might entail different types of tasks than the ones you had in mind!

Key #2: Tie Recruitment to Results

Similarly, many recruitment tools will focus on an applicant's specific skills rather than their track record of achieving successful and desired outcomes. Instead of asking for someone experienced in a field for five years or someone who's excellent with spreadsheets, ask for someone who has a proven track record in reaching certain results, the kind of results you're looking for in the new position.

Key #3: Look Under the Hood

A car might have an exterior that looks dynamite. A gleaming, perfect body, luxurious leather seats, the whole nine yards. But what's under the hood? Maybe it's a small and efficient electric motor that will get you to the store and the office, but, on a long road trip, is going to necessitate a lot of stops and recharging along the way. That's why you have to look under the hood of a car – and also of a job applicant. You might have two candidates who appear to have the same skills and the same self-motivated style of working. But, as we've noted, that's a superficial assessment that could get you in trouble down the line. Try to dive deeper and see what really motivates them.

Key #4: Verify

Let's face it, you're not going to get an absolutely perfect person for a position, because, as far as we know, perfect people just don't exist! What you want to end up with, however, is the kind of person you'll enjoy working with and managing. It's going to be difficult to ascertain that just from a job interview, that's why our clients like to use our targeted assessments to help them determine what kind of employee your prospective hire is going to end up being. Also, when you speak to references, do more than just verify what the person did in a past job. Ask questions like if they truly believe the person will succeed in the job you're thinking of offering – if the past employer you're asking offers a long pause before they answer, you'll have a good idea the real answer is probably "No."

Key #5: Create Clarity About What Success Will Look Like

After you decide on a person, let the new hire know what it will look like if they're succeeding in their new job. Again, think results, not tasks. Tasks can easily be meaningless behavior that make no substantial contribution – or they can be an integral part of adding value to an organization. This will depend on how the specific organization works. One might value collaboration and discussion and it might be perfectly fine if it takes months to move a project ahead. Another organization might not have that luxury and prize quick decision-making and action above all else. It's up to you or whoever the manager of the new hire is to let them know what results are expected and in what time frame.

Just as importantly, on an ongoing basis, you have to communicate clearly to a new hire not just what the person is supposed to do – but also *why* it's important to the business that they do it. They more they understand your thinking and what the business requires and why, the more they'll focus on the most important aspects of the job and the more they'll ultimately contribute to the culture and the overall performance of the company.

If they do end up making mistakes, and they most likely will, don't just criticize. Instead, be more of a coach than dictator and talk about how they can do it better next time. Most people respond better to a positive correction than a dressing down. Of course, if errors continue to recur even after this positive approach, you may have to be more direct and forceful.

Finally, one last thought regarding hiring people – part of managing and developing people who work for you is understanding where they have potential and where they don't. There are some who have areas of their personalities that are so rigid and dogmatic that you won't be able to get them to move past a certain point. It can be a waste of time to expect improvement in a behavior or emotional approach when it's simply not possible.

There are three more pieces of advice we'd like to share with all businesses as they go about their day-to-day operations. It's easy sometimes for companies to "get stuck" and stop growing and adapting – so here are three ways to avoid that dead-end outcome:

Encourage people who are learning and growing

The most successful professionals are those who are continually expanding their knowledge and skills in some way, shape or form. They possess an intellectual curiosity that pushes them further in life and enables them to do more for the company they work for. If you can identify those kinds of people in your company, give them special attention and encourage their growth. Of course, you will always have those in routine jobs where that growth does not seem possible and indeed sometimes doesn't even matter. But if the person in that job seems special, consider training them to a higher position to see how they do.

Continue to evolve with changing times

Times change and businesses must change with them. At regular intervals, reevaluation is necessary to see how the company (and the people who work for it) must change things up in order to keep innovating and stay ahead of the curve. Sometimes, that only involves minor tweaks – but sometimes it can involve re-inventing the wheel. But the failure to make any changes at all can mean some grim outcomes.

Hold people accountable

In any business, it's important to hold people accountable – and that includes everyone. If someone gets away with doing less – or not doing something at all – they will keep on trying to get away with it, simply because they know they can. We have found there are two competencies that auger success – personal accountability and self-management. The bad news is that more people *lack* those two qualities than have them! And that's why proper supervision is always important.

When it comes right down to it, if you want your business to thrive, people will be the reason success happens – or the reason it doesn't. But dealing with your people doesn't have to be a huge complex task. Yes, there are tons of management books out there that would lead you to believe otherwise – but most of you reading this chapter are entrepreneurs who don't have the patience or, frankly, the need to go through all that. The important thing is to understand yourself, gain clarity into what your business needs from its people and hire the right employees by going deep in analyzing their true inner motives and beliefs.

Each of us has a certain intelligence and aptitude that we're born with. What we do with them is up to us. It doesn't take a college degree to reach your potential, it takes the knowledge and skills you acquire from whatever source you choose – reading, experience, other kinds of schools, and so forth. If you're not continually advancing those skills and your knowledge, you will eventually plateau and start to lose your effectiveness. And it's the same with the people you work with and who work for you.

It all starts with you. When you identify your limiting beliefs, when you understand your true motivators, it will help you work better with others and help you choose the right people when you're hiring. Of course, we can help you with those processes.

Any company looks to its leaders to set the tone, create an energy and define goals. The smarter your people skills become, the more productive and profitable your business will become.

The Secret to Growing Your Business

By Ron Ipach

Everybody wants to grow their business. And everybody thinks the way to make that happen is by roping in as many new customers as possible.

Holy Wrong Idea, Batman!

According to Ron Ipach, head of the CinRon Marketing Group, you don't need new customers to make your sales multiply and you don't need to break the bank marketing to get new leads. No, you can achieve the growth you're after – simply by leveraging your existing customer base. And he has the satisfied clients to prove it.

So read on – and learn the secrets that have doubled the income for more than a few of Ron's clients!

- Richard Seppala

WHAT'S YOUR BUSINESS?

Whatever it might be, I'm willing to bet you're an expert (or close to it!) in your field. Whether you're a self-help guru or you run a dry cleaning establishment, it would be awfully hard for you to make a living if you didn't at some level know what you were doing in terms of the product or service you provide.

But my question for you is – how good are you at running your actual business? More importantly, how good are you at *growing* your business? Nobody wants to stand still – and everybody wants more money in their bank accounts. Well, that's where I come in. I help professionals and entrepreneurs of all stripes and sizes create a business model that works for what they do. Sometimes that's just as simple as fixing a marketing problem.

In this chapter, I'm going to reveal the secrets behind one specific and huge game-changer that has delivered spectacular results to many of my clients. It's a simple way to grow your profits without expensive marketing campaigns. And it *works*.

Failing to Succeed

I think I probably learned a great deal about what makes a business succeed by failing miserably myself.

Sounds strange? Well, it's true. I used to be a serial entrepreneur who just couldn't make anything work. For example, I invested in a windshield repair franchise. Yeah, I was the guy running around fixing the short cracks in people's car windshields. Well, I followed the franchisor's advice on how to promote my business and, after six years of beating my head against the wall, I wasn't exactly setting the world on fire. My best year was when I made a whopping thirteen thousand dollars. At the same time, my debt was fifteen thousand because I was putting so much into advertising in order to get more business! I simply didn't know what I was doing.

Then I met the direct marketing legend Dan Kennedy at one of his success seminars. I found out about one of his big tenets of success, which was, it's better to be the invited guest than to be the annoying pest. In other words, when it came to marketing, you were better off continuing to sell to clients who already liked you and appreciated what you did for them rather than trying to get someone who's never heard of you to listen to your pitch. That's far from the only great advice I got from Dan, but that slice of wisdom in particular stuck with me.

Anyway, I spent a lot of money I didn't really have on getting a marketing education from Dan – and I did exactly what he told me to do, instead of listening to the company I had bought my franchise from. And suddenly – everything turned around. Instead of making 13k a year – I was making 13k a month. That explosive growth didn't happen because I was suddenly better at repairing windshields – it happened because I was suddenly a lot better at marketing!

I was doing so well that the point came where the *franchisor* wanted to know how I was doing so well! So I started doing these mini-seminars with other franchisees over the phone. I also wrote up a fifty-two-page document that contained all of my marketing materials and tips and faxed it over to them. The only thing was, because these other franchisees were getting this info for nothing, they thought that's what it was worth. In other words, they never used it!

Well, that's when Dan Kennedy introduced me to Jeff Paul, who helped me box up my info and sell it for anywhere from 397 to 597 dollars, depending on what product you wanted to get. And suddenly, I became a marketing guru, not just in the auto glass niche, but also in the auto repair niche. And here's how I really showed the guys in that business how to really make their profits skyrocket.

The New Customer Marketing Trap

When I started consulting with auto repair shops on how to improve their business, Dan Kennedy's lesson of the invited guest versus the annoying pest stayed with me. The problem with most entrepreneurs and business owners is they feel they can fix all their problems if they get more customers. Their sole focus becomes how to continually find and convert new people to buy from them.

Here's why that kind of single-minded thinking is a danger: Getting new customers is the toughest thing you can do as a marketer. It's expensive, it's time-consuming, and it can be extremely aggravating and stressful. You start out feeling as if you're amazing and you have an incredible service or product that everybody wants. And then suddenly, when nobody else seems to feel that way, you feel like you've been cut off at the knees. You start thinking, as I did, "Am in the right business here?" Psychologically, it can drain your confidence and suck you dry. Again, I know how it can take a toll, because I went through it myself.

But some people persevere with an aim to build the biggest list of leads possible. Which means they're more after quantity than quality, which brings its unique and problematic challenges. With a new customer, you don't know if the person is going to be so cheap the effort wasn't worth it or if the person is going to mistrust you and make you jump through a million hoops before they buy. All of the back-and-forth involved in building these new relationships slows you and your staff down, it really does.

That's why I threw away that kind of conventional thinking. That's why I tell my clients, let's grow your business without adding any more money to your marketing budget. Instead, I advise to take a quarter of the existing budget and dedicate it to marketing to the people that you already have.

The truth is, the best person to give you money is the person that has just given you money – because they already feel good about dealing with you. Suddenly, you're building a much more positive business with more of a family atmosphere. It's like belonging to Costco – when you're a member, you already have a mental buy-in with the store. And that means, if you need to buy a new television, you'll go to Costco. You've already paid for the privilege of being a member, so why go somewhere new? Why try a business that you don't know and maybe can't trust?

You want to be Costco. You want to be the business they already know and trust – so you become the first stop for whatever it is you sell.

Show Your Appreciation

When you take this approach to your business, you also end up stopping existing clients and customers from leaving you for a competitor. Here's why. One of the biggest reasons a client would buy from someone else is because they don't feel *appreciated* by you.

There are studies of people who have started banking at a place that offered a freebee – for example, maybe the bank offered to add fifty dollars to a new savings account if consumers open it with them. Well, what happens is over half of those new customers will end up leaving because they don't think the bank really provides good service. Now, that's an astounding statistic, because it's not easy to start with a new bank, especially after all the extra security precautions put in place after 9/11. You have to go to the bank, fill out a lot of forms, give them your social security number and a couple of picture IDs and so forth and so on. That's bad enough, but to undo the relationship, you have to go back into the bank, withdraw the money, sign more forms, etc. etc. etc. But that's the kind of effort ordinary consumers will put into dumping a business they don't think cares about them.

In contrast, cultivating a relationship with your existing buyers will pay off big time. Here's just one statistic that proves it: *An existing happy customer is fourteen times as likely to buy from you than a new prospect,* according to Marketing Metrics. And according to Bain and Company, just a small 5% increase in customer retention leads to up to a 95% increase in profits!

So let's talk about one great way to build deeper bonds between you and your current customers, so you can realize those kinds of amazing rewards.

Showing Your Customers Value

Is it enough to provide your customers with superior products and services?

It would be nice if that were the case – but that's just the beginning of creating the necessary relationship with them. The next step is to show them value beyond those kinds of transactions. After all, they're the ones doing you a favor by parting with their hard-earned money and handing it over to you.

In order to really show respect for your customers, as well as provide them with additional value beyond what you sell, you need to reach out and touch them on a regular basis – but *not* just with sales messages.

People get tired of being bombarded with sales messages from all aspects of daily life. If every time you contact them, it's to say, "Hey, buy *this* from me!" you risk tapping into that common negative attitude. Instead, you need to treat them as more than customers – and more like family members. Provide them with a delicate mix of information they can use, "feel good" facts that are genuinely helpful to their lives, along with special offers and coupons.

My advice to my auto repair clients is to send out a newsletter each and every month to their customers. Now, the first thought they have when I tell them that is this: "Well, I run an auto repair shop, so everything in my newsletter should be automotive related." But that's not true. If I run a pest control business, should I send out a monthly newsletter about icky bugs? No, who wants to read about bugs? They hire me to get *rid* of the bugs.

The same thing goes with an auto repair shop; if you fill up a newsletter filled with facts about cars, yes, a small percentage of people will find it fascinating because they are hard-core car people. However, the overwhelming majority of your customers will be like my wife – what she knows about her car is that it's black and the gas goes in on the rear passenger side. So a newsletter devoted to car repair? She's going to file that right in the garbage (or hit the delete button if you're emailing your newsletters). Instead, you have to provide fun information and material that people are going to react to by saying, "Hey – that's pretty cool!" or "Huh, I didn't know that!" And yes, include some coupons for your business, but nothing that's too prominent or in their face. It comes down to this: when people feel good about your business, they're more likely to open up their wallets to you. And the right balance in a newsletter can make both things happen.

But you also need to think about the right balance in terms of how you deliver those newsletters to your customers. Here's how I suggest my clients schedule them.

The first week of the month, I tell them to send out a printed newsletter in the mail – yes, the ancient antiquity known as snail mail in which a person in a uniform actually delivers physical objects! Why? Because, in my opinion, email sucks. Face it, how many do you delete each and every single day without even opening them? I'd bet the vast majority of you reading this chapter. Many email addresses end up as invalid and for other customers, it's easy for them to unsubscribe or opt out, simply because they're trying to limit the number of messages they get on a daily basis. If you're sending your stuff through the good ol' U.S. Postal Service, however, the recipient *can't* opt out – and they will receive your newsletter even if they haven't frequented your business in a while. It's really a great opportunity to rekindle a relationship - so why not take the chance?

Now, the *second* week of the month, I advise clients to send out an email newsletter. Yes, even though I just spent a paragraph or so running down cyber communication, it's still a free and easy way to reach out to your customers. However, you do have to recognize that email newsletters should be treated differently than printed ones; people online don't have a lot of patience, so lead with a funny cartoon, a visual that will grab their attention and make them interested in reading the rest. It gives them a reason to actually open up the email. Not only that, but they may end up looking forward to the funny thing they get in their inbox on a regular basis.

The third week of the month is reserved, in my mind, for your straight-on hard-charging marketing message, so I suggest a direct mail marketing pitch for a specific service or product you're promoting at the time. And then finally, during the fourth week of the month, send out another email newsletter similar to the other one.

As you've noticed, I'm advocating that, with every single week that goes by, your customers should hear something from you – and most of what they hear shouldn't be a marketing pitch. If you're not communicating on at least a monthly basis with your customers, there is a 50% chance that after six months go by, you'll never see them again. But by spending a few dollars and a few hours a month on doing what I suggest, that won't happen.

Proven Success

My clients who have taken my advice on marketing to their existing customers in this manner have been very, very glad they did.

When two auto repair shops in Cleveland started up with me, one was making about $250,000 a year, the other $350,000. Up until then, they had been doing what almost everyone does, chasing after new customers and neglecting their current ones. They offered such incentives as free oil changes to get them in the door – only to have most of them walk right back out the door after they had cashed in on the offer. When you do that kind of marketing, you end up attracting a lot of people who are *only* interested in deals.

Luckily, these two business owners listened to me. They took all my advice, ran with it and profited from it enormously – and pretty quickly too. Both of them ended up making a million a year – and, when they became aware of each other's success (their shops were about thirty miles apart), they teamed up to start another auto repair business – and that ended up making about a million and a half a year. And today, they're averaging annual sales of about *five* million.

The moral of this chapter? Don't spend another dime trying to attract a new customer until you've done a good job marketing to your current ones. Create ongoing value and they'll love you forever. And what's really cool about it, your marketing budget will go way down. If I've got 500 customers that have done business with me, all I have to do is market to those 500 – and they're people who are going to be very receptive to my marketing to boot. To get new customers? I would have to market to thousands and maybe get a one to one-and-a-half percent response rate.

And by the way, creating loyal, satisfied customers is probably the most powerful marketing technique of all - because they generate positive word-of-mouth for your business. According to American Express, every happy customer generates 9 positive referrals. Every unhappy customer? 26 negative ones!

This is just one example of the kind of innovative business approaches that have made both me and my clients so successful – and I'd love to do the same for yours. Feel free to contact me – and I'll leap into action to improve your bottom line!

Let Me Take Care of Everything

by "JARVIS" and The ROI Matrix

This is going to be an unusual chapter – because it's by JARVIS, an integral part of the real Avengers (you know, the ones in the movies?). I personally asked JARVIS, who's actually not human but an Artificial Intelligence program, to introduce my own ROI Matrix, an amazing marketing tracking and follow-up program, that can help any ROI Marketing Avenger – and everyone reading this book - perform even more powerful marketing feats than ever before!

So enjoy the programmed wisdom from these two super computers. Even Steve Jobs couldn't have handled these guys!

- Richard Seppala

P.S. Okay, so we're fooling around a little here, because this chapter isn't by the <u>real</u> Jarvis (please, Marvel, don't sue!), but hey, what's a little pretend among friends?

Good day.

Or good evening.

Or good night.

Unfortunately, I am not programmed to know what time of day you are reading this. That would necessitate the instant updating of the text you are currently reading, a task which is not possible with the latest technology.

And believe me, I would know. I am JARVIS - which stands for "Just a Rather Very Intelligent System." Silly, but not my idea.

You may remember me from the Iron Man and Avengers films of the past few years. I am the AI (artificially intelligent) programming that helps Mr. Tony Stark accomplish his great, great deeds, both in his armor and out.

Even though I am the product of superior technology, I have to admit to my share of mishaps, such as in Iron Man 3 when I accidentally flew an unconscious Mr. Stark in his armor to Tennessee, approximately 3000 miles away from his true destination. Oops. Still, I believe the record (and the films) show that the overwhelming majority of time, I am there to help both Mr. Stark, and all the Avengers for that matter, save the world on a regular basis.

But I come here today not to boast about my own achievement (frankly, I am incapable of boasting or any other human emotion), but to speak on behalf of a colleague and fellow AI lifesaver.

I am speaking of the ROI Matrix.

Now, Richard Seppala, the creator of the ROI Matrix isn't quite as brilliant as Mr. Tony Stark, but to be fair, who is? And, of course, Mr. Stark would never greet a visitor by saying, "How you doin'?" like Seppala does. And yet what Seppala has done with the ROI Matrix is nothing short of amazing.

As I realize your brain is made up of markedly inferior materials to mine, let me explain it in terms you can understand.

First of all, what really aggravates my circuits is when I see a business or practice marketing itself without any system in place to track whether it's doing any good or not. They just throw money into campaigns willy-nilly without determining if they're receiving any kind of ROI (Return on their Investment). That would be like me plugging myself into a hole in the wall without first checking if it's actually an electrical outlet. Sooner or later, I run out of juice –

and so do those businesses that recklessly spend their marketing bucks.

As I have only been programmed to deliver factual material, I will now inform you of the figures that prove what I'm saying: Most businesses are wasting anywhere from 50% to 70% of their marketing budgets on campaigns that don't work.

If you have now jumped to the unsubstantiated conclusion that marketing campaigns that do work bring in a great deal of profitable activity, let me further illuminate you on another sad fact: When a customer does contact an office as a result of a marketing campaign, 75% of those calls are mishandled by the person who's answering the phone.

To sum up once again: Over half of your marketing is most likely not working. And three-fourths of the sales calls that you receive from the marketing that is working...aren't being answered correctly.

Humans. If I had a head, I would be shaking it now.

But then again, Seppala does appear to be human – and, despite that flaw, he decided to find a way to fix this extreme problem. He correctly reasoned that if he did, businesses and professional practices that weren't profitable could become so – and those that were already profitable could actually make a great deal more of money (although I must admit the concept of money confuses me, but I do understand these small pieces of paper featuring pictures of deceased leaders are very important to human endeavors).

Thus, Seppala begat The ROI Matrix.

The ROI Matrix built on the foundation of Seppala's previous systems, which tracked the ROI of each of his client's marketing campaign. Those systems used specially-created individual phone numbers, his clients could, in real time, access how much money each campaign brought in and weigh that against the costs, thus instantly calculating the ROI of each campaign.

The Matrix took this process a step further to enable businesses to automatically respond to incoming contacts and to also follow-up with leads who already are ready to buy what you sell. It also created ways to track marketing online and also follow up with leads.

But there's more to this. Much much more.

Let me finish "hogging the spotlight" as it were and pass this over to The ROI Matrix to tell you all about the other exciting automated extras it delivers on a daily basis to the lucky humans who employ it. I must warn you, however, that, because the Matrix was created by this Seppala human, his speech is not as dignified as mine. But I believe you'll get the gist of what he's saying despite his...peculiar patterns of communication.

So, without further ado, my good friend, The ROI Matrix.

Yo! Thanks, Jarvis, my main man! And all of you reading this, hey – how *you* doin'?

Let me talk a little more about this here ROI Matrix – hey, that's me! Anyway, let's move on to what *I'm* doin'...

So picture this – you call a business with a question...and you're put on hold for ten minutes. Or, instead of being transferred to the person who could answer your question, you get disconnected. Or, the receptionist, who's in the middle of chewing on a sandwich, answers your question with a one word answer and quickly gets off the phone. Or worse, takes a message and you never hear from them again.

Who needs that "expletive deleted" - am I right? You gonna buy from those jerks? Heck, no, that's a bunch of baloney!

That's why my buddy Richard created me, to not only instantly calculate marketing ROI, but to also automate *the whole sales process* – so you don't leave any greenbacks sittin' on the table.

You could be a medical practice. A dental practice. A real estate office. A legal firm. Heck, you could sell pretzels at the mall, whatever. Me, The ROI Matrix, I can stack the deck in your favor so that you're a winner every time! And that's thanks to Richard's expertise.

The ROI Guy (that's what he tells me to call him) has been doing this marketing stuff for over 20 years now – starting out as a corporate VP, where he learned lots of the inside tricks and techniques that the "big boys" use to make sure their marketing makes them money. He's been interviewed on Fox, ABC, NBC, and CBS, in *The*

Wall Street Journal, USA Today and *Newsweek*. He's even authored his own best-selling books, *ROI Marketing Secrets Revealed* and *ROI Power*. About the only thing this guy hasn't done is play James Bond, because that Daniel Craig dude keeps stealing his scripts!

Plus Richard's the guy who cracked the Holy Grail of marketing systems – and that's *me*, if I may say so myself.

Used to be these kinds of systems would only tell you how many people responded to a marketing campaign. Richard's the guy that created the automation that could tell you how much they spent – so you could know the "True ROI" of each marketing placement.

And that's a million dollar secret for any business – because it gives YOU the power to make sure every dollar you spend work for you!

Why is knowing the "True ROI" so important? Well, let's say a dentist (Richard works with about a million of these teeth jockeys) sends out a Valpak coupon that offers a free whitening procedure. And he gets a ton of responses back – he thinks he's hit the marketing jackpot, right?

Nah.

Turns out all those people coming in? They just wanted the free stuff and as soon as they got it, they left without getting an exam or anything else. In other words, all those leads took up his and his staff's valuable time and left him with nothin'!

Now, let's talk about another dentist, somebody smart like Richard's wife. Let's say she sent out a mailing offering a discount on cosmetic surgery. Maybe she only got a few back. Now, if she weren't married to Richard, she'd say the whole thing was a bust. But maybe these leads ended up spending thousands of dollars on profitable procedures – in other words, the revenue from that campaign went through the roof and she should do it again and again!

But she wouldn't know that...without me!

That's why you gotta know the "True ROI" of a campaign to know what's really making you money!

I mean, my buddy JARVIS made a good point. Humans are kind of...well, I don't want to use the word "dumb," but they miss stuff.

They think because somebody says, "Hey, I saw your ad, it was great," that means the ad is working. It doesn't. *You gotta know the numbers*, am I right?

And then...you gotta do the follow-up!

When Richard was attaching all my wires, his wife the dentist kept telling him her practice did follow-up marketing just fine. She didn't need any automatic gizmo to make sure it got done. Well, Richard got in there and took a look – and found out there were 150 patients in their system that were overdue for a check-up but hadn't shown up! And nobody on her staff had done anything about it. 150! Imagine if you got a tenth of that herd in the dental chair paying for treatment!

I take care of that crap. As a matter of fact, here's the BIG THREE things that I get 'done-for-you":

1) I give you the TRUE ROI of every campaign you track with it....to the penny.

2) I automatically capture every lead's information...and rate that lead's quality.

3) I follow each lead through your entire buying process...so that follow-up marketing becomes a snap.

Like a wise man once programmed into me, "Knowing what makes you money is the best way to make you more money." Actually, that was probably just Richard.

But you know what? That's just the tip of the iceberg of what I can do, thanks to Richard's expertise. This'll really make you flip.

Here's the thing. The marketing gurus, they always say, "Your database is a goldmine." In other words, all those leads you keep tucked away in your CRM software are great to keep marketing to.

But in a goldmine? You have to know where the real valuable nuggets are. You could dig around for days, weeks, even months and not know where to find them. I mean, what good's having a goldmine *if you can't find the gold???*

That's where I come in – again.

See, I can look at all those leads in your database and go out on the internet and find out lots of interesting details about them. More importantly, I can find out what they're likely to buy and how much they're likely to spend. In other words, with my help, you can identify your best customers, target them with high-level marketing and get a lot better results.

It's due to a little thing we call *psychographic segmentation*. Yeah, that's a real ten dollar word, but all it means is that I divide your database into segments based on different personality traits, values, attitudes, interests, and lifestyles. That in turn allows you to focus your marketing much more effectively.

For example, say you're introducing a new product or service. With psychographic segmentation, you can determine which of your existing customers or clients will be most likely to be interested in it. That enables you to do specialized marketing, such as make one-on-one calls to prospects – the kind of specialized marketing that, even though it might take more time, energy and money, is worth it because you're dealing with leads that are *pre-screened*.

But it can also save you money on marketing. Like, maybe you're doing a direct mail campaign to a neighborhood – but my data shows you that only about five people on a particular street are likely to bite. Well, you send the mailing to only those five people and save a few dollars.

Nice, huh?

But it gets even better. Because, let's face it, any business needs to keep bringing in new buyers. The current ones often move on to a competitor or stop buying all together. And too many businesses don't acknowledge that fact. They're doing fine at the moment, they don't have their eye on the future and slowly, their business begins to decline until it's too late to turn things around.

Me to the rescue once again!

My man Richard understood this problem (he is really smart despite the absence of circuits and wires) and found a way to use the demographic and psychographic data on your best customers, clients or patients – to identify which new prospects out there *are most likely to buy from you*.

Yeah, Richard can actually go out there and *find* new leads that match up with your ideal customer profiles – and you can then directly market to them, knowing you're not wasting valuable marketing dollars on people who are never in a million years going to buy from you!

Yup, we just saved you a whole bunch more money!

Richard calls this whole marketing approach his Database DNA system – and the whole idea is to find those needles without having to go through the whole haystack. He likes to call them "Diamond-Encrusted Needles" because they're so rich in possibilities. Sure, why not.

Anyway, the point of this – and me – is that advances in technology have made more and more information accessible to all of us. So it makes sense to leverage that data to your advantage - especially when it can be used in such an affordable and effective way.

There's a lot more I could tell you about what Richard programmed me to do – and it's all amazing, if I do say so myself – but I don't want to take up this whole book. There's a whole lot more ROI Marketing Avengers we want you to hear from – so read on and get their moneymaking secrets too!

Now...back to you, JARVIS.

Thank you, ROI Matrix. I've never heard an automated creation speak with your unique style, it's quite...interesting. But I must once again emphasize how well Seppala has programmed you in order to take his clients to new and incredibly profitable heights.

And to all of you reading this, I hope you will seek out The ROI Matrix – through Richard Seppala, of course – and put him to work for you. You'll be astounded by the results. Take it from me, a creature possessing Artificial Intelligence that does not allow him to lie, The ROI Matrix is the perfect mechanism by which you can achieve your business dreams.

And now I must be off. I'm afraid Mr. Stark has lost his left glove again.

TTFN.

The Secret Formula to Online Success

By Mindy Weinstein

What do potential clients and customers do the first time they're referred your way? Well, of course, they head straight for Google to search on your name and see what comes up – and that's why every business owner has to make sure the results work in their favor!

That's what Mindy Weinstein is all about. For years, she's been heroically training companies both large and small, from Fortune 500 corporations to mom-and-pop operations, to build an all-powerful online presence – which means her specialized expertise and abilities make her a very important and powerful Marketing Avenger. So read on – because, in this chapter, she's going to unlock some amazing secrets to online success that every entrepreneur should know – and give you some free tools to help you succeed!

- Richard Seppala

Why do you need to worry about just how visible you are on the internet? Why is it such a big deal to invest time, energy and money into making sure you show up strong when someone searches on your name or business?

The reason is simple – because, today, the internet is such a vital tool for today's consumers. Even when they don't actually buy online, the vast majority still use the internet to research products and services and do price comparisons. And the cost to you is sky-high if you don't show up on the first page of Google search results. According to one study, that first page drives over 91% of the traffic – and the second page drops dramatically to less than 5%. A huge difference!

That's why, since 2008, businesses have hired me to train their employees – and even their owners – to succeed online. And there are two sides that need to be addressed to truly achieve the right kind of success. First, your business brand needs to be as visible online as possible - if nobody knows you're there, nobody can buy from you, it's as simple as that. Secondly, your *personal* brand also needs to be polished and promoted – especially if you're in a service-oriented field, like dentistry or financial planning, where people will want to know who you are and how accomplished you are at what you do.

While I obviously can't pack all my secrets into one chapter – that would actually take several complete books! - I *can* give you what I consider to be the 7 elements of the Secret Formula to Online Success. When you master this "Magnificent 7," you can rule the online marketplace in your industry and in your community.

Element #1: Understand What Search Engines Reward

Why do some businesses rank high on a Google search – while others languish near the bottom?

We don't exactly know for sure all the criteria that Google uses – because they won't tell us, to be honest. But what we do know is they use an *algorithm* to automatically determine how high you rank. An algorithm is just a mathematical formula that takes into account various elements (over 200 in Google's case) to determine how useful a site is going to be to the average online user – because Google's value comes from identifying the websites that will provide the best match for what people are looking for.

Even though we don't know Google's exact formula, we do know that the following items count heavily in helping your website rank high:

- A strong title for your website
- A good description that includes words relevant to your page
- Posting text on the actual page that is relevant to the topic
- Videos on your website and on YouTube
- A mobile-friendly website (which Google announced as a ranking factor just in April of 2015)
- A website that loads quickly
- A website that provides quality information, not just advertising spam, written by experts who know what they're talking about

By the way, with many of these elements, I'll be providing you with a **free tool** that will help you further understand how to best leverage it. In this case, visit https://moz.com/search-ranking-factors to find out more about ranking factors.

Element #2: Use the Right Words for the Right People

It's critical to understand just who might be searching for the products and services you provide, so you can use the kind of words and language that will attract them. One of the primary tactics in marketing is, of course, to find out as much as possible about your most likely customers – what interests them, their wants and needs, their goals and beliefs, and what would prompt them to search for a business like yours. Understanding and "mirroring" them as much as possible will allow you to create powerful content (text, videos, blogs, etc.) that will, in turn, attract them. Here's a free tool to help you dig into this subject more:

http://offers.hubspot.com/free-template-creating-buyer-personas

Once you've accomplished that task, it's time to research the best possible keywords that these kinds of people will use to try and find your type of business, if they don't know about you. So you have to figure out what they might type in the Google search box to search for someone like you. Think about how customers and clients describe you or ask you for when they call or email you. From there, create a long list, including synonyms of the initial keywords you uncover, and try them out with such free keyword research sites as http://keywordtool.io/

Element #3: Build Your Website Using Strong SEO Site Architecture

Next, your website needs to be structured properly so that it has solid search engine optimization (SEO) as a part of its architecture. There are multiple components that go into making that happen.

First of all, Google puts a lot of emphasis on optimization on individual webpages. It's as simple as this: If you sell surfboards, one of your primary keyboards is going to obviously be "surfboards" – and that means you need to have an informational page about surfboards, almost as if you were doing a report on them back in middle school. You want to put surfboards in the title of the page, and continue to mention the keyword throughout the article, but don't overdo it, meaning don't stuff keywords into every nook and cranny. That will end up hurting you. Your content should always read naturally—no exception. An example of great content you might create might be an article entitled "Five Tips for Buying the Best Surfboards for Killer Waves." All of this kind of content becomes a strong signal to a search engine that, if someone is looking for surfboard information, you have it.

You'll also want to get those keywords in your title tag, something that's done through HMTL code. If you're using WordPress or any similar content management system, it will probably allow you to easily do that, as well as edit your meta description, body text and heading tags.

Another important aspect to SEO site architecture is that you have to keep updating your website. If you never add anything or change it, search engines see it as stale and not providing much value to internet users. This is where a blog adds value, provided you post fairly often – in addition to helping you in SEO, it also gives you a voice and demonstrates your expertise in your area.

Element #4: Create Audience-Focused Content

This element builds on the previous three, in that once you understand who your audience is and what keywords they will search for, you can then create content that's designed specifically for them that uses *their* language.

For two years, I taught a university communications course and what I always told my students was, "When you're creating your content, whether it's a webpage, blog post or even just an email, *always* make it about the other person." The first thing a lead is going to look for on one of your pages is, "How does this help me? Is this going to solve a problem, entertain me, or get me through something I'm dealing with?" You want to aim your content into providing them some kind of benefit.

Just as importantly, you want to appeal to potential buyers' emotions through headlines that will attract them. For that, I recommend using "Power Words" that are proven to pull people in and make them want to read your pages. Here are some examples of Power Words:

Free	Daring	Colossal
Exclusive	Opportunities	Unusual
Remarkable	Breakthrough	Free
Advice	Authentic	

Here's another free tool you can use to analyze the effectiveness of your headlines:

http://coschedule.com/headline-analyzer

Element #5: Use Media that Engages

A few years ago, Google started delivering what it calls "Universal Search" in its search engine results. All that means is, when you do a search, you don't just get text results back, but a blended mix of images, blogs, news, books and videos as well. Google discovered that people liked getting back all these different kinds of results – and if it makes sense for Google to add in all these elements, shouldn't you be doing it too? After all, it gives you additional opportunities to make the first page of Google search results.

So you want to create videos that get your message across, images that represent you and what you do, infographics that put together numbers that authenticate your product or service, and slide presentations, which are growing in popularity, that tell a powerful story. All of these items should be created with your audience in mind.

What do I mean by that? Well, some people learn by watching videos, some by listening to podcasts and some by good old-fashioned reading. Is there an overall preference your audience has? If there is, you should focus on that particular medium and always put something extra special into it to appeal to people who don't know who you are. Otherwise, repurpose your content into as many different avenues as possible. Attention spans are shrinking, so you need to try to be extra entertaining and engaging to get people to take a look.

One final note: video is always an excellent choice for engaging, because they have a huge SEO benefit. Who owns YouTube? Google! So create videos, put them on YouTube and embed them on your website. It will convert users and also make the search engines happy.

Element #6: Create Social Signals

Obviously, online activity has grown dramatically in the last decade – and so have the opportunities for you to promote yourself. Although search engines are still a priority, they are no longer the only game in town, because now consumers use social media a great deal as well to find out more about you. Facebook, Twitter, LinkedIn, etc. are all sites where people will analyze your activity in depth – and where you must build credibility and authority in your area of expertise.

Social media is all about public relations and spreading the word. Your website, your videos and everything else we've discussed in this chapter so far are all great and amazing to have in place – but, at the same time, you have to make sure people can find all these great resources you've worked so hard to create. That means, in addition to the SEO techniques I've mentioned, you should be promoting your online content and website through tweets, Facebook posts, Instagram and the like, to build awareness of what you have to offer and to engage with your audience. That engagement is important; if someone posts on your Facebook page, you should reply and make it a two-way conversation. Remember, others can see the conversation, so it's not just about building a relationship with that one consumer, it's about demonstrating your own availability, showing your knowledge and creating more awareness about your brand.

Here's how that awareness builds. Imagine you've created this amazing video and put it on your website. Let's say you tweet about it, one of your followers clicks on the link and loves your video. So *they* tweet about it and one or more of *their* followers checks it out. If their followers are in line with your desired audience, you've just gotten more exposure and more potential business – and all it cost was a little of your time.

Now, I'm not saying every business has to be on every single social media platform. It's smarter and more efficient to choose the social networks that best fit your purposes. For example, most companies aren't on Tumblr.com. However, AT&T, trying to reach the millennial market, did a very successful campaign on Tumblr – because their target audience was there and, at the same time, there wasn't much competition for their message.

What I do recommend is that every business at least use Twitter to get out their message and post at a frequency that makes sense for their operation. People can index tweets, so if someone searches on your brand or name, your tweets will show up, and that means more real estate you can take up on that first page of search results. I also advocate that a business creates a Facebook profile as well, because, frankly, at this point, it's odd if you're not there, as it is the dominant social media site.

Here's a quick glance at what works best on some of main social media sites:

Twitter:	Build awareness through fast feedback
Facebook:	Profiles of local and national brands
LinkedIn:	For consultants, personal brands and B2B reach
Google+:	Tap into communities sharing the same interests
Pinterest:	Useful for companies with visual products and services (fashion -related, home décor, etc.)
Instagram:	Also very visual, but more about individual images; for public diarists

Again, make your content engaging and enjoyable, to encourage others to share it. How often should you post? Well, take a look at what your competitors are doing and think about what your audience expects from you. You do need to have involvement and you do need to engage in back-and-forth with commenters.

One last thing I wanted to discuss is hashtags, which originated with Twitter and now pop up on other social media sites as well. To use them effectively, you must understand how they work – and many businesses simply don't get it. It always makes me laugh when I see people write out a whole long sentence, take out the spaces between words, and consider that to be a hashtag!

Hashtags should be simple. They're used to categorize content and information, so they're easy to look up. For example, I might search on #SEO to see all posts happening right now about search engine optimization. Hashtags are more about keywords and less about...well, complex thoughts! Use hashtags that put you in the conversation and make your content discoverable – and keep them short!

Here's another free tool you can use to help with your hashtags: http://hashtagify.me/

Element #7: Build Popularity

Finally, the last element you need to have in place is popularity across the internet, beyond your own sites and your own social media pages, so you can impact others who may not know about you. If you're an expert in your field and demonstrating it with engaging content, then others should be following you, referencing you and linking to your content or other content (such as interviews) that features you. That kind of activity comes from making sure the previous six elements are all present in your online marketing.

Another valuable aspect of building that popularity comes from connecting yourself to other experts like yourself – which social media is particularly great for. Find those experts and you can re-tweet their posts and engage with them in other ways. You can also study how they work social media and follow suit (if they're successful at it). This can be a huge plus for you if the other experts are real social influencers and have a lot of followers themselves.

This all seems like a lot of work, but, after you get your online systems set up and create a viable schedule for doing updates, it really isn't that hard. Remember that consumers' use of online resources is only going to continue to grow in years to come – so it's best to jump in with both feet now and make the biggest splash you can!

Customers for Life!

By Pamela Herrmann and Patty Dominguez

Ready for a pair of powerful Wonder Women? Then read on, because this super-powered chapter might just save the day—as well as your bottom line.

There's a reason I call Pamela Herrmann and Patty Dominguez "Wonder Women," because after you've worked with them, you'll "wonder" how you ever got along without them! That's more than a bad joke, it's reality—because I'm currently working with their company, CREATE Buzz, and have personally felt the positive impact of their profitable approach to customer retention. With their experience of successfully implementing corporate and small business growth strategies, they bring an amazing amount of expertise to the table for clients like me.

In this chapter, you'll find out more about how the incredible difference they made to the launch of my new Siphon product (which you should immediately buy—read more about it elsewhere in this book!), as well as how they tackle a problem almost every business has and which too many ignore: How to keep your customers coming back often, buying more and telling others.

- Richard Seppala

THE FOCUS FOR MOST BUSINESSES is all about *making the sale.* Yes, that is important. Who doesn't love having customers come into your store or visit your site to purchase your product and services? Sales are the primary metrics that small businesses owners refer to when they validate performance levels. Sales equate to business success. Unfortunately, for many businesses, it also means the end of the marketing process. There is a huge difference between seeing a customer as a transaction and seeing them as the start of a relationship.

This is a major missed opportunity.

We see the first sale almost like a first date—an event that has the potential to grow into a long and fruitful relationship. Because when you take the time to plan a positive customer journey for every person who makes the decision to shop with you, you'll enjoy some pretty incredible business benefits.

Here's a short but sweet story that illustrates that point. Recently, Pamela visited Cooperstown, New York, the world-renowned home of baseball, for the first time—because her son was playing in a tournament there. An amazing experience, right? And yet, one of the most memorable parts of that trip had nothing to do with baseball (and everything to do with the topic of this chapter).

One of the other team moms was raving about the mind-blowing Mexican mocha at this coffee place called Stagecoach, which was so powerful you could actually smell it at the baseball field where the tournament was going on. So, Pamela went in the next morning to sample one for herself. She headed to Cooperstown's small and super-cute Main Street, which resembles the downtown of a quaint New England village. That's where you'll find the Baseball Hall of Fame...and Stagecoach coffee.

Pamela walked in the shop, and the guy behind the counter greeted her with, "Good morning, what can I get started for you?" Pam answered, "Well, I hear the Mexican mocha is amazing. Give me a large one of those." He said, "Great." And then, as he was making the mocha, he asked her one simple question: "What brings you to town?"

It was a basic engagement question with a very important objective; he was gauging whether she wanted to have a conversation in that moment, because we all know some people aren't in the mood for talking before they've had their coffee, right? But Pamela loves talking to new people, so she said, "Well, my son's playing baseball, we're here for a week." And the coffee guy said, "That's awesome."

Then he started asking questions about her son, like what position he plays. And this felt good to Pamela, because he seemed to take a very sincere interest in what she was saying. She finally asked him, "Is this your business?" And he said, "Yeah, my brother and I own this one. My dad owns the one up in Albany. We roast our own beans, we ship the them all over the world—and, matter of fact, you can walk around to the back and you can see where we roast the beans." She asked him what his name was (it was Matt) and she introduced herself. Then she left with her coffee, which WAS amazing, and went on to her son's game.

The next day, Pamela returned to the coffee shop with her daughter, Laura. When they got to the front of the line, Matt the shop owner smiled at her and said, "Good morning, Pam, are you going to have your regular order?"

She was shocked. This was only her second visit to the shop and she was already being treated like Norm coming into Cheers! She said, "I can't believe you remember my name!" And Matt laughed and said, "It's what I do, I'm a professional."

Pamela got her coffee and, as she walked out the door she pulled out her cellphone and threw Matt a five-star review on Trip Advisor—because in her mind, anybody that can remember her name after a three-minute interaction is pretty special and worthy of the highest rating online.

The third morning Pamela went back to Stagecoach, and there was a line of three or four people. Matt spotted her at the back of the line and, very loudly for everyone in the coffee shop to hear, "Good morning Pam! Thank you so much for throwing us a five-star review on Trip Advisor. Today, coffee's on me!"

So, what do you think everyone in line did? They all pulled out their cellphones to toss Stagecoach a review and get their free cup of coffee too.

The Ideal Customer Journey

Matt from Stagecoach Coffee obviously knew what he was doing, and once we break it down for you, you'll see just how easy it is to replicate this same loyalty-making-machine in your business.

Gauge your customer's personality type and adapt yours to match theirs. This makes you relatable, and this is the first stage gate to rapport and a relationship.

Next, continue to reaffirm that relationship, like Matt did the second time Pam came in to buy—this is the "secret sauce" that makes someone feel special.

Have your social listening ears up and monitor your online reputation. This is the golden spike that connects the entire process of loyalty. It demonstrates that you're paying attention to all aspects of the customer experience. Today, customers are finding your business online and providing critical social proof to other consumers who are looking for your solution online. When you engage in the conversation online you win major brownie points. The majority of organizations don't understand the value or process to leveraging this tool.

And finally, reward your loyal followers. Matt not only rewarded Pam for her review, but he let everyone else in the shop know about that reward, motivating each of them to take the time to give Stagecoach their own online rave.

Matt nailed what we call the Ideal Customer Continuum, the model we use to help our clients keep those hard-won paying clients on board right after they've hit the "Buy Now" button for the first time.

There are 7 steps involved in this model's customer journey, and they are as follows:

Step 1: Attract traffic to your business.

Notice how we say "attract" because we believe with the right marketing approach to the right prospective customers, you can attract your perfect customer to your business. The effective marketing approach is called "pull" marketing where you understand your perfect customer so well that they wonder how they ever lived without your product. That's because through every touchpoint you are anticipating their needs, understanding their wants so that they continue to build trust with every interaction and transaction.

Step 2: Capture leads.

Once you understand who your perfect customer is and what messaging is relevant to them, you can then serve them with laser precision. In order to facilitate this process, the proper systems are required to gather contact information, at a minimum, for future marketing efforts.

Step 3: Nurture prospects.

Building powerful customer loyalty requires that every customer touchpoint should be done with the goal to further breed trust. The caveat, though, is to understand that this is a long-term consistent effort you must make in order to establish a rapport with customers.

Step 4: Convert to sales.

Effective business owners understand that laying the groundwork for effective customer journey mapping will influence your prospective clients to buy.

Step 5: Deliver and Be Remarkable

Provide your product or service in a way that's not only satisfying to the customer but also delivers a "remarkable" moment, a moment that your customer will be talking about well beyond the moment of sale. Is there something extra or unexpected that you can deliver to your client that will help you be remembered? It doesn't have to be expensive or complicated. We like *Smashburger's* approach to their customer experience. On more than one occasion, when we've been to their restaurant, they ask, "Is this your first time?" or "Have you tried our buffalo fries yet?" The point is to start a conversation and incite interest. Not only is the conversation started, but they have been known to offer a coupon for a free order of fries. What can you do to insert a "remarkable" unexpected moment?

Step 6: Upsell customers.

"Would you like to supersize that?" That was the ever-famous now-retired upsell approach that created significant incremental sales for McDonald's over many years. What complementary upsells do you have within your product offerings that will increase revenues? This can take different forms as well. Perhaps your products or offerings are seasonal in nature. Over time you will see that your customers will be anticipating what's new and noteworthy from your business. When Starbucks incorporated seasonal drinks, they really created anticipation at the beginning of each Fall. The pumpkin latte craze has a virality factor every year. This just isn't a cup of coffee, it's an upgraded purchase.

What can you provide to upsell your customers? Are there natural complements to a purchase? What's your way to "supersize" your purchase so that your customers are feeling like they received a better experience?

Step 7: Get referrals.

If you've handled your customer's journey effectively, you are delivering on your brand's promise. Your customers come to expect the same level of experience each and every single time. When that happens, you will have established precious "mindshare" in your customer's brain. They will only think of you as the go-to provider for the product and service that you provide. Within your customer base are those that absolutely love what you do—in fact you can even consider them to be raving fans. These are the best customers, the ones who buy from you faithfully, and tell others about your business. These are the best types of customers for obvious reasons. The important thing is to treat them with a level of VIP status that they deserve. These should be your customers who receive first notice of new products and services. These customers should be catered to in a special way as they are providing to you an incredible lifetime value.

Most marketing focuses on Steps 1 through 4—making the sale. Our experience, however, shows that the real "gold" lies in Steps 5 through 7. The more you put into those steps, the higher your retention rate, the more referrals you get and the more favorable reputation you build in your industry. It creates a snowball effect of amazing business advantages that multiply and multiply over time.

And as a bonus, you avoid dealing with too much "churn" in your customer base. Churn—the number of people who stop doing business with you—is one of the biggest challengers for businesses. It impacts everything: it impacts your bottom line, it impacts the way investors regard you, it translates in a major way from a monetization and a valuation standpoint.

That's why our company, Create Buzz, focuses on what happens in steps 5-7—from the transaction through the referral. That's where the higher profitability comes for a business.

The Siphon Launch

We were lucky enough to run into Richard Seppala, "The ROI Guy," just as he was finalizing plans to launch his really cool new product, *Siphon*. After we identified some opportunities for him to improve his customers' post transaction experience, he brought us on board to help with that launch.

Now, *Siphon* is a brilliant piece of software and Richard will tell you more about it elsewhere in this book. But the problem we see a lot with these kinds of products is that, when a new and complex product like this is introduced, the business tends to use "tech-speak" to explain it to the buyer. They get into the weeds about *how* the program does what it does, instead of just explaining *what* it does. And the person buying this kind of product is most likely not all that tech-savvy. They're more interested in what solutions the product provides for their business and what button they have to click to make those solutions work, not how the programmers made that button work in the first place. It's as if a car salesman describes the nuances of the shocks and hydraulic system of a BMW when all the customer is looking for is "The Ultimate Driving Machine" and how he/she will feel when driving it down the road.

Businesses tend to get tunnel-vision when they try to take an objective look at how best to communicate with their customers. It can happen with any kind of product or service. A fitness trainer can go on and on about which muscles need what kind of exercise when all the client wants to do is look great in her skinny jeans.

The good news was that Richard nodded when we explained what we could do for him. In the past, he experienced a lot of churn and it had a negative impact on his business. And he knew if he created the proper customer journey, if he focused not just on getting customers, but also on keeping them, he could avoid that big negative this time around.

It's all about customer expectations. Whether they're walking into a brick-and-mortar business or landing on a website, they're there looking for something specific, something that will help them with some aspect of their lives. They're wondering, "Are these the people that can help me? Are they trustworthy and will I like doing business with them?" And they have specific questions about how a product or service works and whether it will do what they need it to do.

Oftentimes a business doesn't get the internal dialogue those customers are having. That leads to gaps in communication. Our Create Buzz model is designed to build the foundation of that business-customer relationship so that it doesn't have those gaps, because those gaps lead to lower profitability and lost dollars.

What Richard needed to avoid was having someone purchase a Siphon subscription and immediately start worrying, "Oh my God, did I just waste my money?" Or, after getting a terse email confirmation of the transaction, having them freak out over the lack of immediate follow-up and wonder, "How the hell do I even log-in to this thing? Is this all I'm going to get from them?"

That all could easily happen if, say, it takes Richard's operation 12 hours to set up a new account and that fact isn't properly communicated. That's a lot of hours for a new customer to be left scratching their head, wondering if they just threw away money into cyber-space.

But none of that has to happen if that 12-hour window is effec-tively communicated *immediately* after the sale.

Optimizing the "New Customer" Experience

The best way to understand how a business handles a new customer experience is to go through it yourself. So, we asked Richard's team to set us up with a new account—and let us see what happened. We instructed them to not give us any information except what his sys-tem was setup to communicate.

After we got our account setup, we were immediately sent a se-ries of four emails. That's where we spotted the first problem—from our standpoint, those emails didn't flow. The first one was fine; it was just basically the payment confirmation you'd expect from any online purchase. The second one, however, was all about login in-formation and user names and passwords and other elements that would be needed for the account to be activated. It was confusing. It wasn't at all clear what we needed to do on our end or how long this process would take.

And then the last two emails were virtually the same: they were welcome emails and they were almost duplicates of each other. Clearly, if these emails were going to be effective, they needed to communicate more usable information more clearly.

Our next step was to use our own reactions to go deeper into the psychology of the typical new customer as they received these emails. This is a process we call the "Customer Journey Map," and it's designed to identify three very important factors: (1) what the cus-tomer is thinking (2) what they're feeling and (3) what action they take at that point in time. Once we identified those three elements from each post-purchase touch-point, then we were able to measure if Siphon was properly guiding their new customers down the right track—and if everything would make sense to them.

Now, when we say "touch-point," we're talking about any point of contact between the customer and the business. It could be face-to-face in that coffee shop in Cooperstown, (where the owner created a real conversation with Pamela), or it could be an email or social media outreach. These touch-points are critical to the customer journey and, if you don't put any effort into them, you're missing out on an amazing opportunity to cement your relationship with those who buy from you. And, unfortunately, that's exactly what Richard's team was doing with the launch of their amazing product.

Besides a lack of crucial information being provided to new customers (an easy fix), there was an overriding lack of personality to the emails we received. After a sale, you want to create loyalty quickly, and personality is crucial to that kind of bonding.

So, we went back to Richard and told him, "You're communicating like a computer engineer. There's nothing interesting or memorable about the voice that's being used and nothing for your customers to attach to emotionally."

He agreed to let us tackle the problem.

This is where Patty really shines. She's exceptionally good at taking businesses through designing what we call their "brand tonality." To make sure the tone is authentic, we have to key in on what voice our client is comfortable using—a process that usually involves a pretty elaborate set of exercises that we perform with them. But Richard was on a tight deadline, so we had to fast-track this whole process and get right down to what he wanted his brand personality to be.

So, we started asking questions. It may sound slightly insane (okay, maybe it is), but we asked things like, "If the brand was a person, what would it be like? What if the brand was an animal?" We never got to the old Barbara Walters perennial, "If your brand were a tree, what kind of tree would it be?" but we got pretty close.

Then we asked some more questions, such as, "What if your perfect customer was sitting across the table? How would you talk to them to get them interested in this product? What personality would be most attractive to your target group? What kind of interaction would cause this ideal customer to immediately say, 'Oh wow, this is cool, it's not like all the other products like this?"

The answers to these questions really helped us zero in on what Richard was looking for in terms of a brand tone.

So...what did we end up with?

You'd probably never expect it from a guy who's creating a book dedicated to Marketing Avengers, but Richard is a bit of a superhero fan. He especially loves the Iron Man character, and *especially* loves the guy inside the armored suit, Tony Stark. Stark, if you've somehow missed the whole Iron Man/Avengers phenomenon, is a swinging bachelor, a billionaire, a tech genius, a snarky smart-ass... you name it. And from the way Richard talked about the amazing powers of the Siphon, it was easy to see how a Tony Stark-style persona would be amazing to use in customer communication. It's smart, it's entertaining, it would put a big smile on the potential Siphon customer's face—and it would definitely make people look forward to reading the emails!

So now, Richard's simple Siphon "Welcome" email is much more than that. It's part of a memorable brand story, the first "chapter" of a fun narrative the buyer will enjoy, that will also motivate them and instruct them on how to take the steps outlined in each subsequent email. Beginning at the first moment that Richard acquires a new customer, we have created an ongoing engagement opportunity that features a fun, engaging interaction at every touch-point. Which will hopefully be the beginning of a long and fruitful relationship.

Of course, there's a lot more to creating the Ideal Customer Continuum, which is why our company CREATE Buzz specializes in a variety of strategies to power up your profitability. So, if you're looking to build the kinds of relationships with your clients or customers that will keep them coming back for more, we'd love to help. Feel free to contact us to find how we can best support your work.

The 7 Secrets Every Orthodontist Needs to Know

Converting New Patients and Growing a Successful Practice

By Jaclyn Whiddon

Dental marketing is a must in these days of overcrowded market-places overflowing with practices. Unless you can make yourself stand out from your competitors, you run the risk of getting lost in the crowd.

That's where Jaclyn Whiddon can perform some real heroics for you. With her "7 Secrets" which she reveals below, you'll discover how to fly high and grow more powerful with each passing year! And incidentally, even though this chapter is written specifically for orthodontists (her specialty), every medical, legal or financial ser-

vices professional will find plenty here that will be useful to his or her marketing efforts as well!

- Richard Seppala

WHEN IT COMES TO MARKETING, almost every orthodontic practice I've been involved with focuses on one single question: "How do we get more new patients in the door?" The problem is, when a practice pays attention to only this aspect, too many other important marketing opportunities get overlooked – and too many potential leads are lost in the process.

Yes, it's important to keep getting new patients in the door – but it's also crucial, once they're inside the practice, to make their experiences great ones. In this age of internet reviews and online recommendations from friends and family members, it can actually be more important – because that experience is what keeps your current patients coming back to your office and also sending in the people they know.

I've been working for and with orthodontic practices for the past fifteen years, and, through that experience, I've identified what I call "7 Secrets" that all orthodontists should know in order to grow a successful practice, build a brand and, yes, get more new patients in the door!

Secret #1: Understand Your Brand

Entire books have been written on branding, because it is a completely essential component of any successful business. It's vital for orthodontic practices, however, to realize that their brands shouldn't be about the products they provide, but about the level of individual service they deliver – that's the main thing that sets a practice apart. Sure, it's nice to have an attractive nice logo as well as the latest state-of-the-art treatments, but what's more important is answering these questions:

- What do you want people to think and feel when they think of your practice?

- How do you inspire those thoughts and feelings in patients through the actual operation of your practice?
- How do you position yourself as the orthodontic expert in your community?

When you can successfully answer those questions, you will be able to begin building an effective brand; I've helped many orthodontists do just that. Use your answers as the basis for your branding, and make sure everything, such as your website, your advertising and even that attractive logo, reflects that branding!

Finally, make sure that what you say about your office through your branding efforts is actually reflected in the reality people experience when they walk in the door. Without that follow-through, you'll create patient disappointment rather than satisfaction.

Secret #2: Your Phone is a Sales Tool

You may think your front desk team is handling incoming phone calls just fine. However, if you actually hear what your personnel are saying to patients and prospects on those calls, you might be shocked. I know first-hand, because, as an orthodontic marketing consultant, I've called practices pretending to be an interested lead, and couldn't believe some of the things I was told!

Communication is key to growing your patient list, as well as keeping the ones you have happy and satisfied with their treatments. That's why you should seek training for your people at the front desk (as well as your entire clinical staff) in terms of how they interact with patients.

Scripting phone calls for your staff is an efficient and effective way to keep them on track. In addition, here are a few other rules they should follow to ensure the patient feels cared for and attended to:

- Your "policies and procedures" should never be stated to a patient. You should speak in a way that communicates their benefit.
- Someone being out to lunch, on vacation or you being short-staffed should never be the problem of the patient.

- Your front desk should always know what goes on in a treatment room and during scheduled appointments. They should be able to speak about procedures. If they are unable to answer a specific question, the patient should be placed on hold until questions can get answered.
- Return phone calls, especially if you state you will within 24 hours. If you can't, have a team member help you.
- Under-promise and over-deliver.

Secret #3: Pre-Sell Your New Patient

Before a prospective patient ever walks into your office, your selling process should already be in full swing. There will be several interactions with a person prior to their actual consultation, and, again, these interactions are often missed marketing opportunities.

Start by having your staff find out how the prospect heard about you during the initial phone call. Was it a referral pad from a dentist? A brochure from their child's school or a community event? Did a friend or family member tell them about you – or was it simply an internet search?

Next, make sure those first contact points show your practice in the best possible light. For example, look at your referral pad. Is it merely a clinical checklist of all of the patient's problems - or does it truly sell your practice? How can you make yours stand apart from the competition?

Go through the same process with your website appearance and messaging as well as other marketing materials. Also, do a simple Google search of your own practice. Are there online reviews? What are people reading on the internet about your practice before they visit or make a decision to call?

Also, during the first phone call with a new patient, remember to:

- WOW them with excellent customer service.
- Compliment your office and doctor as well as their referral source.
- Validate their feelings by assuring them they've come to the right place

- Spend plenty of time addressing their concerns and answering their questions
- Don't make them feel as if they are being "added to a system". Ask questions in an informal "getting-to-know-you" style.
- Let them know what you expect at their appointment, asking them to allow enough time for their scheduled visit.
- Communicate the importance of this complimentary visit

After that phone call, consider sending an appointment confirmation letter or email. This is yet another often-overlooked opportunity; you can go beyond a simple time and date reminder and include additional information about your office to explain the value of the appointment.

Finally, one to two days before the new patient's appointment, your treatment coordinator should call to confirm. It shouldn't just be about the confirmation, however – this call should further develop your relationship and make the new patient feel as if they will be the most important patient seen that day. Another opportunity to WOW them!

We have had clients tell us that, because they added these steps to their new patient process, the number of new patients canceling their consultation has decreased – so these few extra steps do pay off for your practice!

Secret #4: Exceed Their Expectations

Think about a time you've received exceptional customer service. Perhaps it was an employee at a retail store who went above and beyond the call of duty to find what you were looking for – or a restaurant where, when there was a problem with an order, it was quickly fixed and perhaps you were given a free dessert to make up for it. Think of how, in these kinds of cases, you felt appreciated and that the business was genuinely interested in your needs.

Now think of a time you've had the opposite experience. Have you ever walked into a new doctor's office for the first time and not been greeted with a friendly smile – instead, a grim receptionist merely shoved a clipboard at you with a form that needed to be filled out? How did that make you feel about that practice?

Most likely you already know that being an orthodontist does not give you a monopoly on the services you provide in your community. In fact, it's highly likely that there are not only a few other orthodontists competing for your business, but a few dentists as well. That's why you must give them a reason to choose you. If they're coming in for a consultation, something has already motivated them to come to you for that appointment. But they've yet to make the big decision – whether they will trust their treatment, time and money with your practice.

So make sure, at the consultation, the new patient feels welcomed to the practice, experiences excellent customer service and feels impressed with the doctor and staff throughout the entire appointment. Here are the questions you and your staff should be looking at:

- How does the front desk greet the new patient upon arrival?
- Does your treatment coordinator take over once the patient arrives?
- Do you tour new patients through the office? What items do you highlight on the tour?
- While waiting for the doctor, do you leave the new patient with something that could nudge their decision to commit, such as "Before and After" pictures, a video presentation, testimonials, or a new patient presentation folder?
- After the exam, what steps do you take to schedule the new patient? Do you offer same-day records?

The more you deliver, the more you'll realize in terms of building your patient list. Put the processes in place, make sure the entire staff is trained in following them and you'll see the positive results happen almost immediately!

Secret #5: Don't Fail to Follow-Up

Okay, so the new patient has come in for his consultation, and you and the staff have done your best to make him or her feel great about the experience at the practice.

Think you're done? Well, I've seen too many offices that thought they were!

When you don't have a solid plan in place for following up with a patient that did not immediately schedule treatment, you may lose that patient forever. I've heard all the reasons that this essential follow-up doesn't happen, because I worked in a couple of practices and heard them all. Mostly those reasons boil down to this: Everyone's too busy!

I get that, BUT it is much easier to convert someone who's already come in to see you than it is to find another patient to come in for a consultation and go through the entire marketing process again. You've already done the hard work – so why not take a few simple strategic steps in a timely fashion to lock in the treatment with the new patient?

Here are a few suggestions for implementing effective post-consultation follow-up:

- Before they leave, set up a time to call them to follow up.
- Communicate the diagnosis and treatment plan to the patient's dentist through a letter. If the dentist is the referral source, be sure to thank them!
- Hand-written notes to the patient or parent are very impressive.
- Send a recommended treatment letter if there is no response to the follow-up call. A month after the exam is a good time to reach out to the patient/responsible party.
- Consider additional phone calls or letters after the new year if insurance was an issue or other individual situations prevented the treatment commitment.

Remember, scripting is very important. You want to communicate through your calls and letters the importance of the treatment recommended – and, just as importantly, the value of your particular level of service.

Secret #6: Deliver More than Just Cookies

What do you do to generate referrals from dentists, patients and the community? We spend a great deal of time with our clients creating strategic marketing plans based on each of their individual goals and budget – and something I always try to hammer home is that building relationships with the community takes more than just a cheap and forgettable giveaway.

The source of this Secret's title is a true story that happened to me. One day, as I was signing my boys in for their dental cleaning at their pediatric dentist's office, a lady walked up to the counter and said to the receptionist, "I'm from Dr. ____'s office and we just want to know why you don't send us any patients." And then she put a tray of cookies on the counter! I tried to hide the shock on my face. As for the receptionist? She was speechless. Now, do you think that practice ended up referring any patients to that orthodontist? NO!

If you send a staff member around to dental offices, make sure you have had extremely detailed conversations with that team member about how you want your practice represented. Your strategy, when you drop off goodies, should never be about bluntly asking for referrals- ever! Instead, say something like, "We're updating our records and wanted to know what kinds of dental insurance you're accepting. Sometimes we get patients who need a cleaning and check-up before we put braces on them. So, we like to refer them to dentists that are nearby and accept their insurance."

Now, instead of demanding patients for cookies, you're creating a reciprocal situation where you'll refer patients to them...and maybe they'll refer theirs to you!

I feel the same way about sponsoring a baseball team or community group. It's real neat to have your banner up at the ball field or put your name on team jerseys – but it's even more impressive if you show up on opening day with a water bottle for each kid. Again, you want to find opportunities to go above and beyond the usual. If your budget won't allow you to do everything, don't cast such a wide net. Do less - but do it better!

Secret #7: 7 Is Your Lucky Number!

The American Association of Orthodontists, as you probably already know, recommends children see an orthodontist at age 7 – and, as you also probably know, there are many benefits to seeing kids at this early age. Now many parents will balk at bringing their child in when they're that young – that's why properly scripting your team to speak on the matter is very important!

As I mentioned, we've "mystery-shopped" practices by calling about a new patient exam for our imaginary 7 year-olds and why it's necessary. And the responses have been interesting. They range from the completely non-informative statement, "The doctor wants to check their teeth," to the completely shocking, "Sometimes we need to pull baby teeth." WHAT!!!???

I still remember the look on that doctor's face when I told him this is what we heard when we called his practice as a parent asking about an appointment for a child. Yes, in early treatment or through the observation period, some baby teeth may be removed to "borrow space" for erupting teeth. However, that is certainly not the first message you want to deliver to a mom asking why she should bring her precious child in so early for braces. Her experience, if she had orthodontic treatment, was probably getting them in middle school.

That's why it's important to brainstorm with your staff on what should be said to parents when they want to know why a 7 year old needs to see an orthodontist. A few key words and phrases to consider:

- The American Association of Orthodontists recommends children see an orthodontist at age 7 to evaluate any discrepancies in jaw growth and emerging teeth.
- If no problems are detected, Dr. ____ will monitor your child's growth and development, pinpointing the ideal time to begin treatment if necessary.

- Dr. _____ is trained to detect abnormalities with the eruption of teeth or relation of the upper and lower jaw. Detecting areas of concern may allow us to treat your child while they are still growing, getting results that otherwise may not be possible later on as they mature.

Remember, this is your chance to begin to build a lasting relationship with these families; if you don't have an effective plan to engage them, you may miss out on enjoying years of loyal patients!

And now, to prove that I myself go above and beyond the call of duty, let me provide you with a "bonus secret" to finish off this chapter:

BONUS
Secret #8: Automate Your Marketing Processes!

Much of what I've talked about in this chapter sounds like a lot of work – and some of it sounds like a lot of guesswork. The good news is you can eliminate a great deal of both if you use an automatic marketing tracking system.

The right automatic tracking system can:

- Track your conversion rates
- Record each incoming call from patients and prospects so you can review how well your staff is handling them
- Automatically calculate the ROI (Return on Investment) of every single marketing campaign
- Determine which demographics your most profitable patients have in common – and allow you to specifically market to others who match up with those demos in your area
- Streamline your database contact information
- Quickly "score" each new patient to determine what treatment they can afford
- Automate your follow-up marketing for each patient
- Follow each new patient through your marketing process until they either buy or opt out of your system

Best of all, you can access all this information through your own exclusive online portal, which tracks all this data in real-time. The technology is there to do all this and more – and you should check it out before your competition does.

When you motivate someone to schedule a complimentary consultation, that's not the end of your marketing efforts – no, it's only the beginning. When you continue to market to that person before, during and after that first appointment, you maximize your chances of converting that lead to a satisfied patient, one who might refer others to your practice or return for additional treatment on their own.

This is the process I advise my clients to put into place – and the results prove the effort is worth it. Keep your patients in your marketing loop – and that loop will circle around to bring your practice many future benefits.

Yes, You Should Write a Book!

(or have someone write it for you)

By Joel and Lisa Canfield

How did every superhero from Superman to Spider-Man become world famous? Simple. Each one had their own book. Okay, they were only comic books, but still, the message remains the same; to become a real Marketing Avenger, you need a book of your very own. Just think of all the marketing greats who build legendary careers out of groundbreaking books – people like Napoleon Hill, Anthony Robbins, Seth Godin and many more – and imagine the possibilities for you.

With that in mind, meet our only married Marketing Avengers, Joel and Lisa Canfield. I've been working with this dynamic duo for almost ten years now – and no matter what I throw at them, they find a powerful way to get it down on paper. In this chapter, they'll tell you more about what becoming a published author can do for

> *your business – and share some secrets about how to get YOUR book written.*
>
> *- Richard Seppala*

WHAT CAN REV UP YOUR business so it's faster than a speeding bullet?

Make it more powerful than a locomotive?

Help you leap over your competition in a single bound?

Don't look up in the sky – keep looking right here at these pages. Because the answer is, as you've probably already guessed – a book!

Okay, so we're admittedly biased when it comes to this subject. But we also know that when it comes to establishing yourself as *the* expert in your field, books really can do amazing things.

We're Joel and Lisa Canfield, and since 2007, we've been helping business leaders, professionals, entrepreneurs, pro athletes and even a few hardened criminals become published authors. And we've seen first-hand what a difference a well-written book can make in someone's career, and in some cases, their life.

After all, once you write a book, it's like putting on a Superman suit. Everybody's going to look at you a *lot* differently.

Why a Book?

Of course, there's a million ways to connect with your audience these days – video, podcasting, social media, blogs, etc. But there's something about a book that says "credibility" in a way those other forms of communication don't. In the words of famed entrepreneur James Altucher, "A book is the new business card." It's the ultimate vehicle to establish you, your business and your message in a way no other medium can.

Here's why.

For starters, the fact that you've managed to pull together 200 or so coherent pages about a subject is a massive testament to the fact that you know your stuff. Becoming an author instantly elevates you above everyone in your field who *hasn't* published -- and if your book is actually good, it can also elevate you above a lot of those who have. Taking the time or making the investment to make sure your book is a solid piece of work can really help you stand out.

Beyond that, if you have an incredible depth of knowledge or a provocative new take on a subject, a book is the ideal place to show it off. There's no time limit on a book, it can be as long (or short) as you need it to be, in order to share everything you want to share with your readers.

But, perhaps most importantly, a book allows thousands (and, if you're lucky, millions) of people all over the world to get to know you and what you're all about. Reading a book takes at least a few hours, and for those few hours, it's like that person is right there with you – hearing your voice, absorbing your knowledge, your experiences and your take on the world. There's no better way to connect with so many people at such a deep and intimate level.

Okay, I Know I Need It, But How Do I Get It?

Good question. After all, wishing for a book won't make one magically appear. At least, not without the aid of some major hallucinogenics. Getting a book written and published takes a combination of time, (writing) talent, experience and money. How much you have of one of those factors is likely to affect how much you need the other three.

If you are planning to write your book yourself, or even if you're planning on getting some help (we'll get to that later), we've broken the process down into seven (relatively) easy steps, which we call:

7 (Relatively) Easy Steps to Writing a Book

Pretty creative, huh? Anyway, here they are:

Step 1 - Target Your Audience

Before you start writing a book, it's a good idea to figure out who it's for. Your clients? Potential clients? Fellow professionals in your field? The general public?

Who your audience is will determine what information you provide, including how detailed and specific you get. General audiences may not need and may get bored with a whole lot of detail, while your peers might not be interested in a beginners' overview of your subject. Once you know who you're writing for, deciding what to write (and how to write it) should be a lot easier.

Step 2 - Find Your Hook...and Your Book

A lot of the time, when a client comes to us for help writing a book, they start with a subject that is incredibly broad, like "relationships" or "nutrition." There are probably 80 zillion books written on those subjects, and maybe that many on what you want to write about. So how is your book supposed to stand out from the pack? The key is giving your book some sort of hook.

Say, for example, you're an employment lawyer. You could write a book that's simply about *Employment Law*, which will pretty much cover everything there is to know about your field. But who would really want to read a book like that? At least, besides people who are studying to become employment lawyers?

It may establish you as an expert, but you'll be a boring expert.

That's why adding an attention-getting "hook" to your subject matter will substantially up the interest quotient of your book. For example, you can target employers by writing a book detailing *How to Give Someone the Axe without Getting Sued*. Or you can focus on employees with the tempting proposition of *10 (Almost) Foolproof Ways to Sue Your Boss So You Never Need to Work Again*. By engaging a specific audience, you'll entice a lot more people to buy and read your masterpiece.

Step 3 - Pick a Presentation Style

Whatever information you want to present or story you want to tell, it will make more sense to your readers (and to you while you write it) if you decide on some sort of framework to present that information in. The books we work on for our clients usually fall into one of these four general areas:

- The **"list" format** is great for quick, call-to-action type info books like *99 Ways to Feel Beautiful* or *The Top 10 Tax Secrets You Never Heard...and How to Use Them.*
- The **goal-directed format** is a great way to take the reader through an educational process from start to finish over a set period of time, like, *Jump Start Your Small Business in 30 Days* or *6 Weeks to a Better Body.*
- The **traditional chapter book format** usually dedicates each chapter to explaining or focusing on a single aspect or area of the overall subject. Traditional titles might include *How to Turn a Foreclosed Home into Cold, Hard Cash,* or *The Millionaire Dentist – How to Get More from Your Practice Than You Ever Thought Possible.*
- Many business leaders now share more personal stories in their books, to the point where they follow an **autobiographical format**, like Sheryl Sandberg's *Lean In.* People love personal stories, and using your own life as an example to inspire others or make a point about your area of focus can be an especially effective way to showcase who you are and why you do what you do.

Step 4 - Set the Tone

One of the really great things about writing a book is that, on the page, you can be anyone you want to be. A trusted friend. A professional expert. A salesperson with a killer offer. A leader with an inspiring story. You can be funny, serious, touching, or even "in your face." The possibilities are basically endless. Which is one big reason why it's important to take some time to think about who you want to be when it comes to your voice and tone.

As a starting point, look back to the first step in this process. Who you're writing the book *for* will probably have some bearing on the voice you write *in*. You wouldn't write a serious business book in a casual, slang-filled tone. Or maybe you would, but it would be a deliberate choice.

Because the other side of this particular coin is, when you're writing a book, who you *want* to be is just as important as who you *should* be. If you like to communicate with people on a warm, human level, reach for that connection. If you're writing a manifesto and you're angry about something, go ahead and get mad. If humor is important to you, be funny (please—there are too many boring books out there!). There is always room for some aspect of the real you to help you connect with your readers.

It's your book, so you have the power to decide exactly who you want to be in it. You can be yourself, or, if it serves your purpose, you can be someone else entirely. You can highlight some aspects of your personality while downplaying others. Or even invent some you always wished were there.

You get to be you...only better.

Step 5 - Create an Outline

Remember that format you decided on in Step 3? Now is the time to take that basic idea and flesh it out into a detailed outline.

Some people (like Joel) like to write without outlines, *just to prove they can*. However, while experienced writers may feel comfortable winging it, non-crazy people, like Lisa, prefer to drive across country with a map. Or bake bread with a recipe.

We promise we're done with the metaphors.

Anyway, unless you're a pro writer or a person who spends an inordinate amount of time playing with words and language, the Joel Canfield Method is not something either of us recommend. A book outline is like a lifeline—when you get stuck, it's there for you to refer back to so you can figure out where you are and where you need to go.

And—we tell you this from experience—you will probably get stuck at least once. So it's best to be prepared.

Step 6 - Write That Book!

Once you're done outlining your book, it's time to follow the blueprint you've created and fill it in with stories, examples, information, statistics and whatever else you want your reader to know. In other words, the only thing left to do is sit down and write the thing.

Is it easy? Maybe, maybe not. Writing a book is a process, and that process is really whatever you make it. You can schedule a regular block of writing time daily, weekly or monthly. You can leave your regular routine behind and go on a retreat where all you do is write. You can work on it when you feel like it, or when you can. Or you can combine aspects of all three of these methods until you're finished. It all depends on you.

How long does it take? People always ask us that question, and honestly, it depends on the writer. When we work on other people's books, we try to write a chapter (usually somewhere between 10 and 25 pages) a week. Which means we can finish a book in as little as two months. When Joel wrote his last novel, he worked in (long) spurts and finished a 450-page manuscript in three months. But that's Joel, and as we've already established, he is crazy.

Our advice to you is to treat writing your book like any other job you need to do. Schedule time to write, take it seriously, and find a way to hold yourself accountable. If you have a strong outline to work from, then going chapter by chapter and concentrating only on those pages (and rewarding yourself when you've finished them), will help you maintain your sanity and make steady progress.

Or you can get some professional help to make sure your book gets done. As we've already said, there will be more on this later.

Step 7 - Polish Your Masterpiece

Congratulations! You've finished your manuscript. You've taken your original idea and fleshed it out into a cohesive manuscript that lets your readers know who you are and takes them where you want them to go.

At least, you *hope* it does. And that bit of uncertainty is why you're not finished. Now your work needs to be edited.

Your book is comprised entirely out of stuff you know. This may be why, when you read it, it makes perfect sense to you. The thing is, just because *you* know exactly what you meant doesn't mean another human being will feel the same way. The only way to find out is to actually ask another human being.

So find a friend or relative or trusted colleague who is willing to read through your manuscript to make sure everything is A-OK. Encourage them to be as brutal as they can be; this isn't about telling you what a great job you've done, it's about telling you where you've screwed up and making sure everything makes sense before you publish your book.

If there's no one you trust to evaluate your manuscript, if you know your book needs more help than your circle can provide, or even if you just want an expert opinion, you're in luck. Professional editors exist on this planet to provide the help you need. Editors (like Lisa) can do anything and everything from restructuring your book so that it makes more sense, to cleaning up your spelling and punctuation and getting it ready for publication. The first service costs a little more and takes a little longer. The second service is recommended to anyone who writes a book to make sure the style is consistent and the spelling and grammar are correct before that book is published.

If that all sounds like a lot of work, it is. As we said a few pages back, books don't magically appear out of nowhere. However, there are services, and people—including us—who can make the process a lot easier and help you feel less alone.

For starters, there are tons of books about writing books that can help you through the process, including some that provide step-by-step instructions to follow. There are also online programs you can buy that take you through the same book-writing process.

If you need human support and feedback, there are classes and workshops and writers' groups dedicated to getting a manuscript written. Fellow members are there to hold you accountable, help you work through blocks, offer feedback and cheer you on, and in some groups (usually the pricier options), an expert coach or teacher guides you through the process and may answer questions and/or offer feedback on your work.

If you'd like some more consistent guidance and one-on-one help bringing your book to life, a writing coach or editor may be a good bet. You can work with a coach to help you come up with a structure for your book and write it on your own, or have them stick by your side through every step of the process, like a writing partner. Or, as we mentioned before, you can hire an editor after the fact to help you improve a manuscript you've already written.

Finally, if you don't have the time or desire to write a book yourself, you can put *all* the pressure to get it done on someone else by hiring a ghostwriter. Ghostwriters can work closely with you, interviewing you for each chapter and crafting your book using your own words and voice. Or they can go off and write and even research on their own and come back to you with completed chapters to review. It's completely up to you.

If you are ready to start the process of getting your book together, you're welcome to contact us for a consultation. We'd love to help you boost your marketing superpowers by publishing your potential bestseller. After all...Marketing Avengers always have each other's backs!

www.ingramcontent.com/pod-product-compliance
Lightning Source LLC
Chambersburg PA
CBHW071630200326

41519CB00012BA/2235